# TWENTIETH CENTURY VIEWS

The aim of this series is to present the best in contemporary critical opinion on major authors, providing a twentieth century perspective on their changing status in an era of profound revaluation.

Maynard Mack, *Series Editor*
Yale University

# MODERN
# BLACK
# POETS

## A COLLECTION OF CRITICAL ESSAYS

Edited by
*Donald B. Gibson*

Prentice-Hall, Inc.  *Englewood Cliffs, N.J.*

A SPECTRUM BOOK

*Library of Congress Cataloging in Publication Data*

GIBSON, DONALD B    comp.
    Modern Black poets.

    (Twentieth century views) (A Spectrum Book)
    CONTENTS: Gibson, D. B. Introduction.—Redding,
J. S. The new Negro poet in the twenties.—Randall, D.
The Black aesthetic in the thirties, forties, and
fifties. [etc.]—Bibliography (p.    )
        1. American poetry—Negro authors—History and
criticism. 2. American poetry—20th century—History
and criticism. I. Title.
PS310.N4G5        811'.5'09        72–12811
ISBN 0–13–588392–X
ISBN 0–13–588384–9 (pbk)

10  9  8  7  6  5  4  3  2  1

PRENTICE-HALL INTERNATIONAL, INC. (*London*)
PRENTICE-HALL OF AUSTRALIA, PTY. LTD. (*Sydney*)
PRENTICE-HALL OF CANADA, LTD. (*Toronto*)
PRENTICE-HALL OF INDIA PRIVATE LIMITED (*New Delhi*)
PRENTICE-HALL OF JAPAN, INC. (*Tokyo*)

# Acknowledgments

We would like to thank the following authors and publishers for their permission to quote from their works:

To the Broadside Press for quotations from *Don't Cry, Scream,* by Don L. Lee (copyright © 1969 by Don L. Lee); *Homecoming,* by Sonia Sanchez (copyright © 1969 by Sonia Sanchez); *We Walk the Way of the New World,* by Don L. Lee (copyright © 1970 by Don L. Lee); *Black Judgement,* by Nikki Giovanni (copyright © 1969 by Nikki Giovanni); *Black Feeling, Black Talk,* 2nd. ed., by Nikki Giovanni (copyright © 1970 by Nikki Giovanni); *Poems from Prison,* by Etheridge Knight (copyright © 1968 by Etheridge Knight).

To Twayne Publishers, Inc., for quotations from *Harlem Gallery,* by Melvin B. Tolson (copyright © 1965 by Twayne Publishers, Inc.); *The Libretto for the Republic of Liberia,* by Melvin B. Tolson; *Selected Poems of Claude McKay* (copyright © 1953 by Bookman Associates, Inc.).

To Dodd, Mead & Company, Inc., for quotations from *Rendezvous with America,* by Melvin B. Tolson (copyright 1944 by Dodd, Mead & Company, Inc.; renewed 1972 by Ruth S. Tolson).

To The Viking Press, Inc., for quotations from *God's Trombones,* by James Weldon Johnson (copyright 1927 by The Viking Press, Inc.; renewed 1955 by Grace Nail Johnson. All rights reserved); *St. Peter Relates an Incident,* by James Weldon Johnson (copyright 1913 by J. Ricordi & Company; renewed 1941 by Mrs. James Weldon Johnson. All rights reserved).

To the Yale University Press for quotations from *For My People,* by Margaret Walker (copyright 1942 by the Yale University Press).

To October House, Inc., for quotations from *Selected Poems,* by Robert Hayden (copyright © 1966 by Robert Hayden); *Words in the Mourning Time* (copyright © 1970 by Robert Hayden).

To Robert Hayden for quotations from *Heart-Shape in the Dust* (copyright 1940 by Robert Hayden); *A Ballad of Remembrance* (copyright © 1962 by Robert Hayden).

To Brandt & Brandt for quotations from *John Brown's Body,* by Stephen Vincent Benét (Holt, Rinehart and Winston, Inc.) (copyright 1927, 1928 by Stephen Vincent Benét; renewed 1955, 1956 by Rosemary Carr Benét).

To New Directions Publishing Corporation for quotations from *Personae,* by Ezra Pound (copyright 1926 by Ezra Pound).

To Faber and Faber Limited for quotations from *Collected Shorter Poems,* by Ezra Pound.

To Corinth Books for quotations from *Preface to a Twenty Volume Suicide Note,* by LeRoi Jones (copyright © 1961 by LeRoi Jones).

To Alfred A. Knopf, Inc., and Harold Ober Associates, Inc., for quotations from *The Panther and the Lash,* by Langston Hughes (copyright © 1967 by Arna Bontemps and George Houston Bass); *The Dream Keeper and Other Poems,* by Langston Hughes (copyright 1932 by Alfred A. Knopf, Inc.; renewed 1960 by Langston Hughes); *Selected Poems,* by Langston Hughes (copyright © 1959 by Langston Hughes).

To The Sterling Lord Agency, Inc., for quotations from *The Dead Lecturer,* by LeRoi Jones (copyright © 1964 by LeRoi Jones).

To *Black World* and Carolyn F. Gerald for quotations from "The Black Writer and His Role," by Carolyn F. Gerald (copyright © January 1969 by *Black World*).

To Liveright Publishing Corporation for quotations from *Cane,* by Jean Toomer (copyright 1951 by Jean Toomer).

To Sterling A. Brown for quotations from *Southern Road* by Sterling A. Brown (copyright held by the author).

To the National Urban League, Inc., for "No Images," by Waring Cuney, and "Poem," by Helene Johnson.

To Harper & Row, Publishers, Inc., for quotations from *On These I Stand,* by Countee Cullen: "Incident" and "Yet Do I Marvel" (copyright 1925 by Harper & Row, Publishers, Inc.; renewed 1953 by Ida M. Cullen); "From the Dark Tower" (copyright 1927 by Harper & Row, Publishers, Inc.; renewed 1955 by Ida M. Cullen); "To Certain Critics" (copyright 1929 by Harper & Row, Publishers, Inc., renewed 1957 by Ida M. Cullen); from *Color,* by Countee Cullen: "To My Fairer Brethren," by Countee Cullen (copyright 1925 by Harper & Row, Publishers, Inc.; renewed 1953 by Ida M. Cullen); from *The World of Gwendolyn Brooks:* "children of the poor," (copyright 1949 by Gwendolyn Brooks); "The Anniad" (copyright 1949 by Gwendolyn Brooks); from *Selected Poems,* by Gwendolyn Brooks: "Rider to the Blood-red Wrath" (copyright © 1963 by Gwendolyn Brooks Blakely).

To International Publishing Company, Inc., for quotations from *New Black Poetry,* ed. Clarence Major (copyright © 1969 by International Publishing Company, Inc.).

To The Bobbs-Merrill Company, Inc., for quotations from *Black Magic Poetry 1961–1967* (copyright © 1969 by LeRoi Jones).

To The Ronald Hobbs Literary Agency and LeRoi Jones for quotations from *Black Magic Poetry;* from *Black Fire,* ed. LeRoi Jones and Larry Neal (N.Y.: William Morrow & Co.): "Prayer to A White Man's God," by Charles Anderson (copyright © 1968 by Charles Anderson); "If you Like Them Wouldn't You—," by Kawasi Balagan (copyright © 1968 by Kawasi Balagan); "The Song of Fire," by Rolland Snellings (copyright © 1968 by Rolland Snellings); "Black Warrior," by Norman Jordan (copyright © 1968 by Norman Jordan); "An Angel Prayer," by Lefty Sims (copyright © 1968 by Lefty Sims), by permission of The Ronald Hobbs Literary Agency and the authors.

# Contents

*For JoAnne, David and Douglass*

# Introduction

## by Donald B. Gibson

### From Poetry by Black Writers to Black Poetry: A Brief History

In its form and content the poetry of black Americans has been
as varied as the multiplicity of personalities who have contributed
to its development. Traditionally it has had no particular core—
that is, it has not been a unified poetry in the sense that the poetry
of the English Renaissance or Romantic periods was unified. This
has been the case except during relatively recent times of great social
stress—in the twenties, for example, and in the sixties and early
seventies—when a genuine black poetry has emerged. During such
times there have been numbers of black poets writing from a more or
less commonly shared perspective on the nature and function of
poetry. At other times, in general, the poetry of black poets has
closely followed the direction of the poetry of the larger culture. In
form it has not differed from the forms employed by poets of the
majority culture; in content, as suggested above, its nature depends
upon the prevailing social and political climate, a factor in large
part responsible for the emergence of the most significant phenomenon in American letters today, a definable black poetry.[1]

Poetry by black writers is either racial—employing subjects, lan-

---

[1] There is a good deal of writing pertinent to this subject. Thrusts toward
definitions of black writing were made in the twenties with Langston Hughes'
"The Negro Artist and the Racial Mountain," *Nation*, 122 (1926), 692–94 (re-
printed in *Five Black Writers*, Donald B. Gibson, ed., New York: New York
University Press, 1970, pp. 225–29) and in the thirties with Richard Wright's
"Blueprint for Negro Writing," *New Challenge* (Fall 1937), 53–65. More recent
"blueprints" are: LeRoi Jones, "Myth of a Negro Literature" in *Home: Social
Essays* (New York: William Morrow and Co., 1966), pp. 105–115 and Larry Neal,
"And Shine Swam On" in *Black Fire*, LeRoi Jones and Larry Neal, eds. (New
York: William Morrow and Co., 1968), pp. 637–56. See also the section titled
"Poetry" in *The Black Aesthetic*, Addison Gayle, ed. (New York: Doubleday and
Co., 1971), pp. 175–262.

guage, attitudes, and scenes from racial experience; or nonracial—
oriented toward experience that is common to the majority of people; or, in varying degrees, both these at once. Generally considered,
it has no more specific character than poetry as a whole. Some black
poets have written racial protest, poems protesting against discrimination or other forms of racism. Some have written about black life
and character, describing it or commenting on it in unprotesting
fashion. Still others have written poems from a completely nonracial
perspective, poems indistinguishable from those written by nonblack
poets. There are no terms or categories which will specifically distinguish the writing of black poets from that of others. Black poets
have tended to be conservative—until recently they have rarely de-
parted from traditional poetic form and style—but even this is not
a distinguishing characteristic, since there are many exceptions and
since they are not, in this respect, unlike many other poets who are
likewise conservative.

The earliest known black American poets, Lucy Terry, Jupiter
Hammon, and Phillis Wheatley, were of the seventeenth century,
and their poems were constructed on contemporary models. Lucy
Terry (1730–1821) wrote a brief narrative poem describing an Indian
raid, a poem important not so much for its aesthetic as for its historical importance. The poem, "Bars Fight," was written in 1746 or
thereabouts and is the first poem known to have been written by a
black poet. A simple, doggerel poem, it is likely to appear uninten-
tionally humorous to a modern audience because of its awkward
rhymes, its archaic language, and its unsophisticated juxtaposition of
ideas.

> Eunice Allen see the Indians comeing [sic]
> And hoped to save herself by running,
> And had not her petticoats stopt her,
> The awful creatures had not cotched her,
> And tommyhawked her on the head. . . .

Whether Lucy Terry (later Mrs. Abijah Prince) wrote other poems
we do not know.

Jupiter Hammon (1720?–1806), a Long Island slave, wrote poems
primarily of a religious, moral character. Conservative in his thinking and devoted to early Methodist piety, he intended his poems
to be moral guides. As might be expected, he was hardly original,

either in form or content. His first poem, "An Evening Thought: Salvation by Christ with Penetential Cries" (1760), is based on the Methodist hymn, and in its thought and language echoes hundreds of other such pieces. He knew of our third earliest poet, Phillis Wheatley, and in fact wrote an address to her as traditional in language and thought as any of his other poems.

Phillis Wheatley (1753?–1784) is the best known early black poet. Born in Africa and stolen from there at about the age of eight, Phillis turned out to be something of a prodigy if we consider that after sixteen months in her new homeland, she was able to read the most difficult texts, and that after only six years in America she wrote "To the University of Cambridge in New England," an eloquent testimony to her thorough mastery of the language, a mastery greater than that of ninety-nine percent of her contemporaries. Her first published poem appeared in 1770, and her first volume of verse, the first to be published by a black American writer, appeared in 1773 with the title *Poems on Various Subjects, Religious and Moral.* Her poetry, by no means original or highly imaginative, nontheless reveals a thorough grasp of the diction and form of conventional neoclassic verse. Like so many of her contemporaries, she was content to follow the practice of the master of the heroic couplet, Alexander Pope, who seemed to her to have defined the very essence of poetry.

There is little allusion to race in Miss Wheatley's poems. Except for a few such references, one would not know her racial identity. This is so in part because she followed the tradition of impersonality so characteristic of neoclassic verse. Her tendency was to cast her feelings in traditional molds so that, whatever might have been her personal, private feelings as a black woman living during the second half of the eighteenth century in America, they remain unspoken in her poems. Her religious inclinations are also responsible for her silence on personal matters. So devoutly religious was she that she undoubtedly felt the poetic expression of faith to be far more significant than the expression of personal concerns. If she led a relatively easy life as the slave and house servant of a Northern owner, as there is reason to believe she did, she might not have felt a strong enough tension between herself and the society about her to elicit expressions of protest. Her marvelously good ear and her capacity to create clear and logical poems were used to promote what must have seemed to her the highest good, Christian faith, even though her later life was extremely miserable and culminated in her death at the age of thirty-one.

During the nineteenth century several other black poets appeared, among them George Moses Horton (1797?–1883?), Frances E. W. Harper (1825–1911), James Madison Bell (1826–1902), and James M. Whitfield (1823–1878). Each of these poets is to some degree political in his use of poetry, writing against slavery or other wrongs perpetrated by society. Horton's first volume, *Hope of Liberty* (1829), was written with the actual hope that it would earn enough money to allow him to purchase his freedom. In it he describes the evils of slavery, thus becoming the first black poet to complain openly about them.

Frances E. W. Harper was the most widely known of this group because of her general involvement in reform, especially the abolitionist and temperance movements. A large number of her poems are devoted to revealing the horrors of slavery, "The Slave Mother" and "The Slave Auction" being among the best of these. Like her black contemporaries and forebears in poetry (and like American poets generally during this time), she wrote in conventional ways about the same subjects that interested many others. She wrote, published, and republished her poetry throughout the nineteenth century; her *Poems on Miscellaneous Subjects* (1854), for instance, exceeded twenty editions.

But Miss Harper, widely known as she was, does not begin to match the accomplishments of a black poet born in Ohio toward the last quarter of the nineteenth century, Paul Laurence Dunbar (1872–1906). Dunbar was the first black poet to achieve national recognition, which was sustained throughout his brief creative life. Dunbar wrote two kinds of poetry, dialect poetry and poems (as he liked to think of them) "in standard English." He considered his nondialect poems his best work and eventually wrote in dialect only because it was demanded of him by editors and the public to whom he frequently read his poems during reading tours. His dialect poems are nearly all about black life and character, and though they are too frequently based on stereotyped characters or situations, from time to time they strike a note of truth when the poet comes upon a phrase, a situation, or a sentiment whose intention is not simply to amuse or to support the prejudices of his white audience. Such elements occur in "A Negro Love Song," "When Malindy Sings," and "An Antebellum Sermon."

Generally romantic, conventional in style and subject matter, and often derivative (Dunbar was steeped in poetry of the past), the poems "in standard English" have not been as well remembered as those in dialect. He would probably have been a better poet had he been able to be more personal, to speak freely and openly of his actual thought and feeling instead of saying conventional things in conventional ways. He is best when he takes off the mask of the poet and speaks as a breathing organism—as in (ironically) "We Wear the Mask" and "Ere Sleep Comes Down to Soothe the Weary Eyes."

Dunbar wrote in all three of the definitive poetic categories mentioned at the beginning of this essay. He wrote dialect poems intended to evoke general human response ("Little Brown Baby" and "A Death Song," for example), though he did not, with the possible exception of "We Wear the Mask," write nondialect poems about black experience. This results from his rather rigid idea of what constitutes poetry—of what subjects are suitable for poetry and what poetic form is. Had he been less rigid, his work might have been more forward looking, though no poet other than Stephen Crane was writing in very unconventional ways at the same time.

The poetry of Leslie P. Hill (1880–1960), George Marion McClellan (1860–1934), and William Stanley Braithwaite (1878–1962) is poetry with a nonracial perspective, reflecting the general experience of the majority culture. Its primary end is beauty, though Hill tends to be philosophically inclined. By far the most accomplished of these poets is Braithwaite, who was widely known during his time as an anthologist and promoter, through his annual collections of magazine verse, of the so-called New Poetry movement. Braithwaite was perhaps the first black writer to set out consciously to be a poet and not a *black* poet. A sophisticated practitioner of the art of poetry for its own sake, he wrote the most successful poetry of this kind before Robert Hayden later in the twentieth century. Another early twentieth-century poet worthy of brief mention is Fenton Johnson (1888–1958), who, following the modes set forth by the New Poetry movement, wrote untraditional poems largely pessimistic in character. His "Tired" is an example: "Throw the children into the river; civilization has given/us too many."

Aside from the present, the period of the Harlem Renaissance, between 1920 and 1930, saw the greatest intensity of creative activity ever to occur among black artists. For once, there were large numbers of black writers living in the same place (Harlem), visiting there, or otherwise in contact with one another. The time was one of great social agitation because of the large-scale black oppression after World War I and the multiple migrations of black peasants from the South due to economic causes. The Malcolm X of the twenties —that is, the most central, cohesive force uniting black people—was Marcus Garvey, who advocated the establishment of a new black nation on African soil to which black Americans would emigrate. No one knows the exact extent of his following, but he commanded the allegiance of very large numbers of black people (some have made estimates in the millions). Although no major poet writing during this time was specifically his follower, the salient point is that through his black nationalist teachings, Garvey was responsible for a greater sense of unity among black people than had ever existed before. The comparison with Malcolm X is an apt one, for the influence of the later leader has extended far beyond those whom he influenced by direct contact. Garvey provided the spirit of the age among black poets and others.

In general cultural terms the twenties was a time when Americans tested the moral and social restraints sanctioned by traditional standards of conduct. Freud had filtered down to capture the popular imagination, and traditionally puritan American attitudes about sex were called into question. It was in this context that the Harlem Renaissance existed. For many white Americans the black man became a fitting symbol of uninhibited, natural, noninstitutional behavior. In order to be whole and fully human—so ran the reasoning of great numbers of whites—one must throw off the restraints of culture and civilization and regain the primitive simplicity of black people. This resulted in a new attitude toward an old stereotype, an attitude no less reprehensible, however, for being new. Many whites imitated black people, but there was always the implication that blacks were by nature uncivilized, amoral, and unhampered by social responsibilities. Instead of simply laughing at the stereotyped black man, the new deal now was to become that man; yet in doing so you resolved that the man could not, or should not, become you. The result of such thinking was to reduce the black man to a set of terms fitting the psychological needs of nonblacks.

In practical and specific terms, this line of thinking meant that black life and culture assumed great importance. Whites began coming to Harlem nightclubs in droves. Musical shows about black people—"Chocolate Dandies," "Shuffle Along," "Brown Rhythm"—became popular. Eugene O'Neill wrote *The Emperor Jones;* Sherwood Anderson wrote *Dark Laughter,* Carl Van Vechten wrote *Nigger Heaven,* and DuBose Heyward wrote *Porgy and Bess*—all white writers, seeing the black man as they wanted and needed to see him.

Black writers used this situation to attain their own ends, though unfortunately they sometimes exploited the situation by writing in terms of the white stereotype. When they avoided this pitfall, the result was the exploration of thoughts, attitudes, and ideas from the inside, from the black perspective. Hence, during the twenties there arose the first large-scale manifestations of black pride: concern for the beauty of blackness, interest in black history and culture, and political awareness of poetry as a means of exploring and celebrating blackness.

Foremost among such writers is Langston Hughes (1902–1967), who has perhaps the greatest reputation (worldwide) that any black writer has ever had. Hughes differed from most of his predecessors among black poets, and (until recently) from those who followed him as well, in that he addressed his poetry to the people, specifically to black people. During the twenties when most American poets were turning inward, writing obscure and esoteric poetry to an ever decreasing audience of readers, Hughes was turning outward, using language and themes, attitudes and ideas familiar to anyone who had the ability simply to read. He has been, unlike most nonblack poets other than Walt Whitman, Vachel Lindsay, and Carl Sandburg, a poet of the people. He often employs dialect distinctive of the black urban dweller or the rural black peasant. Throughout his career he was aware of injustice and oppression, and used his poetry as a means of opposing or mitigating them. Two early poems, "The Negro Speaks of Rivers" and "I, Too, Sing America," testify to his abiding hope for the fulfillment of the American ideal—not only for black people, but for all the dispossessed of the land. Until the time

of his death, he spread his message humorously—though always
seriously—to audiences throughout the country, having read his
poetry to more people (possibly) than any other American poet.

Claude McKay (1891–1948), Countee Cullen (1903–1946), and
Jean Toomer (1894–1967) have an orientation toward poetry somewhat different from that of Langston Hughes. All tend, though in
different degrees, to view poetry as having more concern with the
rhythmical creation of beauty than with the affairs of the world
(though Hughes too wrote some lyrical poems having no social bias).
McKay was very much involved in politics, but that interest finds
limited expression in his poetry. For the most part, he writes about
love, nature, religion, places he has visited, about his home in Jamaica, and about America. Among this group of poets he is the most
like Hughes in that he has written a number of poems whose content
is social, the best-known being "If We Must Die." Other such poems
are "America," "The Lynching," and "The White House."

Countee Cullen and Jean Toomer, though both addressed themselves occasionally to social matters, are by no means social poets.
Cullen has an especially good ear for metrics and finds himself more
at home with Keats, Shelley, and Tennyson than with contemporaries writing experimental verse. Most of his poetry is indistinguishable from that of nonblack poets, though he wrote some poems with
racial subjects or themes. Jean Toomer's case is a much more interesting one, for though he considered aesthetics as the proper end of
poetry, he created in his poetry and prose a mythical black past to
which he explored his connection. As Toomer seems to have sought
the roots of race in mysticism and aestheticism, so his relation to
blackness seems more of the imagination than of the blood. He
translated imagined black experience into forms so idealized as to
be little related to reality as commonly conceived.

The thirties was a relatively barren time for poetry—Sterling A.
Brown (1901–    ) published his *Southern Road* in 1932, using dialect for its realistic rather than humorous effects—and it was not
until into the fifties that a significant number of well-considered
black poets began publishing their volumes of verse. These poets,
Melvin Tolson (1900–1966), Robert Hayden (1913–    ), Margaret
Danner (19?–    ), Gwendolyn Brooks (1917–    ), and Margaret
Walker (1915–    ), are all, like their predecessors of the twenties,
college educated, though (generally speaking) more highly educated

formally. All have been strongly influenced by academic tastes and practices, Gwendolyn Brooks and Margaret Walker perhaps less so than Tolson, Hayden, and Danner. The latter three have written verse which by academic standards is very good poetry, but which might not be easily intelligible to all. Miss Brooks and Mrs. Walker write less esoterically and are closer in this sense to the practice of Langston Hughes. These poets have all competed successfully with their nonblack contemporaries, as the prizes and awards they have won for their poems indicate (Tolson, for strange and complicated reasons, has yet to be fully recognized). Each of these writers is primarily and by profession a poet—not, like many poets of the past, one who writes poems on occasion.

## Black Poetry and Black-Poetry Writers

The great social stress of the sixties has brought about the creation for the first time of a significantly definable black poetry. It is a poetry clearly distinguishable from that written by poets of the majority culture—specifically and essentially urban in character—and different, too, from poetry written by previous generations of black writers. It is a poetry which has its own history and its own character. Its language, form, and style, its intentions and its meaning, have been called into conjunction as the result of the impingement on certain minds and sensibilities of forces peculiar to the modern (especially the industrialized) urban environment. Its patron saints are Langston Hughes and Richard Wright; its high priest is Amiri Baraka—previously known as LeRoi Jones.

Countless poems written by black writers, as noted before, are indistinguishable from those written by non-black poets. Such are some of the poems, as suggested above, of Margaret Danner and Arna Bontemps and many of the poems of Countee Cullen. Likewise, there are many racial protest poems by black poets which are not what we would call essentially black poems, since racial protest as generally conceived is not limited to the poetry we are discussing. There are also poems by black writers which are admixtures of black poetry and more conventional modern poetry. And finally there are poets who write both black poems and conventional modern poems either at different or during the same periods in their careers. Before going further, then, we should define black poetry.

Black poetry is ideological. It specifically supports black nationalism, black consciousness, black cultural and institutional ideals—any or all of these; and its support may be direct or indirect. A specific poem may be about the beauty of blackness, or it may urge its audience toward some action; but in no case is the poem an end in itself, nor is its chief end (to quote Wellek and Warren) "fidelity to its own nature." Unlike most other modern poetry, it is consciously and explicitly didactic. It is also ideological in its attack on existing institutions and social attitudes. Its treatment of sexuality is a case in point. Highly irreverent toward conventional notions of sex and sexual morality, black poetry tends to be very free in its dealing with the sexual act and in its use of sex-oriented Anglo-Saxonisms. Language scatological in nature is allowable as another means of expressing the poet's desire to escape the restraints of the system of institutions and conventions which oppress him. Yet, despite a surface lack of concern with morality, black poetry is highly moralistic, attempting to convince its audience of the meaningfulness and significance of a moral order superior to that reflected in American institutions or that revealed through the attitudes and practices of the society at large.

Black poetry intends always to be as clear, frank, and explicit as possible. It is a poetry of statement, which may engage in puns of an uncomplicated sort, but which intentionally avoids understatement, irony, or complex verbal expression of any subtlety. By being open and explicit, black poetry avoids highly symbolic or complex metaphoric expression, though simple symbols and metaphors may appear. Whenever any of these literary devices do appear, they are sufficiently opaque to be clear to all members of the poet's audience.

This explicitness, this forthrightness, openness, and directness, are in great part the result of the poet's measure of his audience. Although most published black-poetry writers are college educated, they do not write essentially for a college-educated audience, as do most modern poets; nor do they write for other poets. Their audience is the urban mass, and the level of their writing is pitched accordingly (not condescendingly, however) in the interest of communication by means of a medium easily available and well known to both the poet and his audience. Given his ideological bent and his political purposes, the black poet addresses the masses, for he finds the possibility of group solidarity to exist in the working class rather than in the black middle class, a class with which he may at best feel a secondary sympathy and identity. He likewise wishes to avoid the implication of elitism which inheres in the practice of poets who write for professors and other poets, and who for whatever reasons are abstruse or obscure.

Because of the character of his audience, and again because of his intentions, the black-poetry writer uses a language that is colloquial, heavily tinged with slang, greatly dependent on tone, and more Anglo-Saxon than Latinate. It is basically a Southern black dialect (retaining many of the characteristics of such a dialect, especially the vowel sounds) but has been modified by the influences of the urban environment, predominant among which is the intermingling of a variety of Southern black dialects. Thus, its rhythms come directly out of the language rather than being imposed on it by extrinsic principles of rhythmic organization. The apparent "poetic" effects —onomatopoeia or consonance, for example—are likely to be effects preexistent in the language as it is ordinarily used. Its use of artifice is indeed minimal.

Black poetry's use of the language of the ghetto is not only a means of expression consonant with the poet's aim to communicate with people of a certain socioeconomic level; it is also an expression of a complex of attitudes and feelings. The language of the black urban ghetto is used to emphasize unity, commonality of experience, identity. We all know how meanings can be carried by the level of language one uses—implications of class, social and economic status, education, intelligence, sensibility. In the same way, a certain language has come to be identified with black experience, with commitment to certain goals and ideals; and this language, with its nuances of meaning, its conscious difference from standard English, its renaming of things and events (its recasting of experience into its own terms), gives unique character to the poetry.

The language of black poetry has another quite significant dimension: it is a language intended to be spoken rather than privately read. A great deal of this material goes dead when it is captured on the page, because the poet is an oral poet. This follows of course from the fact that he is writing for an audience that is not by and large a reading audience, and that on the whole has little time or inclination to read and whose level of education would not predispose it toward habitual reading, especially of poetry. The poet's assumption is not that his audience will ponder his lines, will read and reread, but that they will instead hear the poem, perhaps only once, and must comprehend it fully during the process of perception.

A great deal of black poetry is intended to be heard in the context of a stage presentation in which mood, rhythm, and tone are enhanced by drums or other instruments, by lighting, and even by the dress of the poet and other performers. Such poetry represents a complete reversal of the expectations of the private poet who displays in his verse his own peculiar perceptions of the world, his own sensibility and sensitivity. Black poetry, by contrast, recalls the communal nature of poetry. It indicates the poet's desire to use his poetry in a way suggestive of religious ritual, though I do not wish to suggest that it is specifically religious in orientation.

Although black poetry tends to be anti-Christian, often in a quite explicit fashion, certain of its qualities seem to derive from the black Christian church. The poet in his reading or performance assumes a role not unlike that of the black preacher, and the audience becomes his congregation. The poet frequently becomes the exhorter, the interpreter of things, the namer and definer. He tells the truth, describes things as they are, and his authority is unquestioned. Frequently there is an interplay between the poet and audience whereby the poet elicits response from his audience either by direct address or by restatement of sentiments or ideas commonly agreed upon. The audience falls back upon a familiar tradition and responds much as it responded when it was a congregation. The response will not be "Amen" or "Bless Jesus" but "Right on" or "Tell it, brother." The old bottles remain; the wine is new.

The forms of black poetry spring from its character and function. Quite free, it seldom restricts itself to rhyme or to regularity of metre. It is cadenced verse, and its line is more frequently tied to natural speech pauses than to formal patterns. Its emphases and its stresses are usually those of natural black urban speech, or else they are determined by a style of delivery common among these poets, a style based on a particular way of stylizing black urban speech. Its freedom from the restrictions of traditional structure matches its general antitraditional bias and its attempt to establish its own particular nature. The number and variety of inventions in form and style may well be the best reflection of black poetry's iconoclastic spirit.

## Black Poetry's Socioeconomic Context

We have asserted the existence of something here referred to as a black poetry. Let us add a discussion of its historical and socio-economic context to support the contention that it is indeed a *black* poetry.

Black migration from the South to the North since before the Civil War (referred to above in relation to the twenties) is a well-known phenomenon. Over the years the numbers of black people migrating to urban areas have consistently increased, and these numbers have been determined largely by economic oppression in the South in conjunction most often with opportunities that seemed (and sometimes actually were) better in urban centers. As larger numbers of black people moved to the cities, several significant things happened. First, black institutions were modified by the urban environment. Habits of speech, dress, and manners were significantly altered. Ultimately—and this of course required a good deal of time—the black urban community took on a distinct character, determined not only by the pressures of an urban environment, but also, and more specifically, by the amalgamation of different black groups from different places in the South who met and interacted in the city. There is probably a generational factor of significance as well, since second and succeeding generations of urban black families undoubtedly tended to be influenced in greater degree by the character of the black urban environment.

Although the poverty, injustice, and oppression inflicted on black urban inhabitants have been quite justly pointed out—and must continue to be pointed out—it is worthwhile to notice that not all black urban inhabitants were crushed by the city. Not all were downtrodden, poorly educated, despairing, and without resources. Those migrants to the cities who were themselves poets or whose children became poets have, in fact, been middle class either in fact or in orientation. Of the poets participating in the two eras most productive of work by black poets, the twenties and the sixties, the large majority have been college educated. The best known younger black poets writing today are both college educated and urban born or bred. To this add the fact that the centers of poetry have been in both periods northern urban—not southern rural. This suggests several relevant generalizations. We may say, first of all, that black migration has been responsible for producing a northern, urban, college-educated group with the leisure, ambition, and desire to use time and energy in writing poetry. Thus, there exists a true relation between geographical, socioeconomic factors and the creation of poetry by black writers. Further, the fact that such groups did not arise previously—that the writing of poetry by black writers was sporadic before the twenties and not centered in specific locales —suggests several socioeconomic corollaries: 1) black urban dwellers did not have the resources to produce significantly large numbers of poets; 2) the general economic situation was not conducive to black gains on a large scale; 3) black migrants were not firmly enough established in sufficiently great numbers to create homogeneous communities. Once communities became relatively homogeneous and once it became possible for some members of the communities to think about things other than the basic necessities of life, it became possible for a few individuals to write poems. This does not account entirely, however, for the existence of a *black* poetry, for the circumstances I have described also produced poets who are black but who do not write the kind of poetry I have described here. So we must take into account additional factors and influences.

Black poetry has developed out of the black thrust of the fifties toward economic and social freedom and equality, and its history is inextricably bound up with the history of that movement, especially as the latter has fostered black nationalism, a concomitant militance, and a pride in blackness not unlike that of the earlier thrust during the twenties. A complete history of black poetry would have to contain references to this larger sociohistorical context, for its dependence on this context distinguishes it from the poetry of black poets written within a more general (Western or American) tradition. Black-poetry writers (unlike black poets) relate directly to the black movement, and though they may not be black nationalists in terms of formal commitment to particular political alliances, they are nonetheless (unlike most black poets of the Harlem Renaissance) committed to a particular view of the function of their poetry. The black-poetry writer draws upon the facts of black urban life to nourish a feeling of community in blackness, and it is this perspective and objective that distinguish him from other black poets.

I see four additional major influences on black poetry: 1) the Harlem Renaissance of the twenties; 2) the protest writing of the thirties as reflected in the work of Richard Wright; 3) the beat movement of the fifties; 4) the life and work of a single poet, Amiri Baraka. It is my impression that most black-poetry writers know the history of black poetry and consequently are familiar with the period of the Harlem Renaissance. Although most of the poets I have in mind probably would agree with Amiri Baraka in his repudiation of that poetry (and perhaps in varying degrees with his nearly total rejection of the black literary past),[2] the Harlem Renaissance has undoubtedly had a great influence on black poetry. Primarily it has provided the image and example of the black poet seriously devoted to his craft. All black-poetry writers know the work of Langston Hughes—perhaps the major poet of the Renaissance—himself, in many respects (as suggested above), a poet who wrote specifically for black audiences, for the common people, and from an ideological perspective, and who can thus be called a black-poetry writer. Hughes has been highly regarded among black writers.[3]

Richard Wright,[4] coming as he did out of the thirties, has conveyed to the black-poetry writers something of the spirit of dissent, a dissent strident, vigorous, and unapologetic in its expression. He provided by example the tone of a great deal of black poetry, exemplified superbly in the title of Don L. Lee's *Don't Cry, Scream.* Unlike both Hughes and Wright (and many other writers of the twenties and thirties), the black-poetry writers avoid social protest of the sort that is directed to the hearts of the nonblack majority. Their work sometimes protests, but it is not a protest requesting redress of grievances.

From the beats of the fifties the black-poetry writers caught the spirit of iconoclasm and social criticism. They learned the possibilities of uniting poetry and music and, as well, the potential of the poet as public performer and of the poem as public gesture. Many

---

[2] See LeRoi Jones, "Myth of a Negro Literature," footnote 1.

[3] In a poll conducted by *Negro Digest* (since become *Black World*), vol. XVII (January 1968), some forty black writers voted Langston Hughes the second most important black writer of all time.

[4] In the poll referred to in note three Richard Wright was voted the *most* important black writer of all time.

of the social ramifications of the beat movement have been carried over into the black-poetry writer's conception of poetry and the poet. Amiri Baraka is the main link here, having been associated earlier with several of the beats.

Baraka is generally recognized today not only as the first articulater of the requirements for a black literature but also as a kind of spiritual leader of black-poetry writers. Although it seems to me that he has had great difficulty in adhering to his own theory of what black poetry should be, he has nonetheless pointed the way for younger poets. During the late fifties and early sixties, he was a very successful contemporary poet and playwright, whose verse, though unique in its way, was not unlike that of other academic poets: complex, obscure, written primarily for academicians and other poets. After a period of transition, traceable in his poems and essays, he turned his back on the established powers responsible for making him a success, and set about working toward the organization of the black community in his hometown, Newark, New Jersey. His poetry underwent several significant changes (as did his name from Jones to Imamu Amiri Baraka), becoming aggressively militant in its tone and message, and directed, in the manner of Langston Hughes, to the people. Most of the younger black-poetry writers have followed his lead. The strength of character shown in repudiating an established career as a very good poet and playwright—the peer of those recognized as the best—in order to follow the dictates of his own conscience must be admired no matter how his subsequent life and work are judged.

The black poem, then, is the child of the city. Its creators begin with the proposition that poetry must be used in the struggle to overcome oppression—a proposition which, needless to say, has historical precedents. The proposition is not in itself urban in character, but it has been put forth in an urban environment and as a corollary to other events occurring in the cities. It is of necessity intertwined with the context in which it has arisen. Hence, the character of black poetry is a function of its social and historical sources. Its form, style, and content are limited by the boundaries of Western culture and civilization; yet within those boundaries it has carved out a character, defined by its particular aims.[5] Never

---

[5] Examples of black urban poems may be found in *Black Fire* (cited above). I call attention especially to the following poems: "Prayer," p. 191; "Index,"

before has there been any significant body of literature by black writers so closely resembling a uniquely black literature.[6]

p. 194; "Revolution!!" p. 196; "Announcement," p. 202; "to all sisters," p. 255; "Now the Time," p. 265; "Burn," p. 269; "My Brother," p. 271; "Election Day," p. 296; "Black Art," p. 302; "Sinner," p. 390; "It is time," p. 420; "Brother Harlem," p. 447.

Some of the better known writers of black urban poems are Don L. Lee, Ted Joans, Mari Evans, Sonia Sanchez, Etheridge Knight, Nikki Giovanni, and, of course, LeRoi Jones. Let me point out, however, that not all the poems of these poets are necessarily "black" poems.

[6] See Donald B. Gibson, "Is There a Black Literary Tradition?" *New York University Education Quarterly*, II (Winter 1971) no. 2, 12–16.

# The New Negro Poet in the Twenties

*by J. Saunders Redding*

The new Negro movement in literature began with a West Indian Negro. Claude McKay had already published a few dialect pieces when he came to the States in 1912, drifting from Tuskegee to Kansas and on to New York. His first years in New York were concurrent with the early social thinking that had been stimulated by reason of the war. Working in an editorial capacity for the *Liberator* and *The Masses*, he must have felt the liberal currents that swept through the pages of those journals; but his infrequent poems gave no hint of his own social thinking. Even the volume *Spring in New Hampshire* reveals more of the conservative poet of nature than of the bitter revolutionary of a few months later. But his gifts stand out in that volume—his love of color, his lush imagery, his sensitive massing. The sometimes indefinable difference that marks the work of the new Negro writer is evident throughout *Harlem Shadows* and especially in such pieces as "Harlem Shadows," "The Harlem Dancer," and "The Tropics in New York."

> Bananas ripe and green, and ginger root,
> Cocoa in pods and alligator pears,
> And tangerines and mangoes and grape fruit,
> Fit for the highest prize at parish fairs,
> Sat in the window, bringing memories
> Of fruit-trees laden by low-singing rills,
> And dewy dawns, and mystical blue skies
> In benediction over nun-like hills.

"The New Negro Poet in the Twenties" (editor's title). From J. Saunders Redding, *To Make A Poet Black* (Chapel Hill: University of North Carolina Press, 1939), pp. 93–125. This essay appeared originally as "The New Negro: The Twenties and Before." Reprinted by permission of the author and the publisher.

> My eyes grew dim and I could no more gaze;
> A wave of longing through my body swept,
> And, hungry for the old familiar ways,
> I turned aside and bowed my head and wept.

It was Mr. McKay's third volume of poetry, *Harlem Shadows*, that attracted his darker audience most. In this volume he gives voice to the violence and bitter hatred that marked the interracial strife of the period just after the war. The proud defiance and independence that were the very heart of the new Negro movement is nowhere so strikingly expressed in poetry as in "To the White Fiends" and in "If We Must Die," already quoted.

Despite the awakening of a new artistic consciousness, however, there was at first much confusion in the new Negro movement in literature. The great tide of feeling which found release was not directed through one channel. While Claude McKay spat out his proud impatience, a few were indulging in slapstick, trying in song and story (and with the aid of certain popular white writers) to restore the older tradition to a state of health, and other writers were groping with curious shyness through the teeming byways of racial thought and feeling, searching for an alchemy, a universal solvent for transmuting the passions of the day into something sweeter than bitterness, more pure than hate. They were for the most part older writers who had an hereditary confidence in the essential goodness of man, in the theory of American democracy, and in the Victorian notion that

> God's in his heaven;
> All's right with the world.

They were of the comfortable middle classes, the bourgeois, school teachers, the wives of pork-fattened politicians and ministers, the sons of headwaiters and porters, spiritually far removed from the sources of new race thought. McKay, Toomer, Hughes, and the numerous lesser ones who came later were vagabonds, as free in the sun and dust of Georgia, in the steerage of tramp steamers, in the brothels of Lenox Avenue and the crowded ports of the Orient as in the living rooms of Strivers Row. These poets were the reservoirs through which pumped the race's hate power, love power, lust power, laugh power. The others, the conservatives, were tubs without depth, within whose narrow limits no storm could be raised. They posed

themselves questions: Am I not just as well as I am? Must I be proud
and glory in my race? And they sought to answer them.

> We ask for peace. We, at the bound
> Of life, are weary of the round
> In search of Truth. We know the quest
> Is not for us, the vision blest
> Is meant for other eyes. Uncrowned,
> We go, with heads bowed to the ground,
> And old hands, gnarled and hard and browned.
> Let us forget the past unrest,—
>      We ask for peace.
>
> We will not waver in our loyalty.
> No strange voice reaches us across the sea:
> No crime at home shall stir us from this soil.
> Ours is the guerdon, ours the blight of toil,
> But raised above it by a faith sublime
> We choose to suffer here and bide our time.

But the bourgeois could not restrain the flood tide. In 1923 came
Jean Toomer's *Cane*, a revolutionary book that gave definiteness to
the new movement and exposed a wealth of new material. A youth
of twenty-eight fresh from the South when *Cane* was published, he
held nothing so important to the artistic treatment of Negroes as
racial kinship with them. Unashamed and unrestrained, Jean
Toomer loved the race and the soil that sustained it. His moods are
hot, colorful, primitive, but more akin to the naïve hysteria of the
spirituals than to the sophisticated savagery of jazz and the blues.
*Cane* was a lesson in emotional release and freedom. Through all its
prose and poetry gushes a subjective tide of love. "He comes like a
son returned in bare time to take a living full farewell of a dying
parent; and all of him loves and wants to commemorate that perish-
ing naïvete." [1] Hear how he revels in the joy and pain, the beauty
and tragedy of his people:

> Pour, O pour that parting soul in song,
> O pour it in the sawdust glow of night,
> Into the velvet pine-smoke air tonight,
> And let the valley carry it along.
> And let the valley carry it along.

[1] Paul Rosenfeld, an essay on Toomer in *Men Seen*.

O land and soil, red soil and sweet-gum tree,
So scant of grass, so profligate of pines,
Now just before an epoch's sun declines,
Thy son, in time, I have returned to thee,
Thy son, I have in time returned to thee.

In time, for though the sun is setting on
A song-lit race of slaves, it has not set;
Though late, O soil, it is not too late yet
To catch thy plaintive soul, leaving, soon gone,
Leaving, to catch thy plaintive soul soon gone.

O Negro slaves, dark purple ripened plums,
Squeezed, and bursting in the pine-wood air,
Passing, before they stripped the old tree bare
One plum was saved for me, one seed becomes

An everlasting song, a singing tree,
Caroling softly souls of slavery,
What they were, and what they are to me,
Caroling softly souls of slavery.

Great splotches of color and sensuousness make gaudy palettes of his
pages:

A feast of moon and men and barking hounds,
An orgy for some genius of the South
With blood-hot eyes and cane-lipped scented mouth,
Surprised in making folk-songs from soul sounds.

*Cane* was experimental, a potpourri of poetry and prose, in which
the latter element is significant because of the influence it had on
the course of Negro fiction. Mr. Toomer is indebted to Sherwood
Anderson and Waldo Frank for much in his prose style, but his
material is decidedly his own. Sometimes he falls short of his best
abilities for lack of government, as in the story "Kabnis," which says
and does much but obscures much more. Sometimes he succeeds
splendidly, as in the sketches "Carma" and "Fern," in which feeling
and language are restrained and genuine. But often he wallows in
feeling and grows inarticulate with a rush of words.

Though *Cane* was in the nature of an experiment (the conclusion
to which we are fearful of never knowing, for since 1923 Toomer has
published practically nothing) it established the precedent of self-
revelation that has characterized the writings of Negroes on all levels

ever since. At first completely absorbed in fulfilling his opportunity for release, the new Negro had no time for new forms. In his anxiety and relief he did not reflect that he was pouring new wine into old bottles. In truth, he was somewhat distrustful of his new place in the sun. He was afraid of being a fad, the momentary focus of the curiosity of dilettantes, charlatans, and student sociologists. It was common sense for him to attempt to establish himself on something more solid than the theatrical reputation of Florence Mills or the *bizarreries* of what many people thought to be the Greenwich Village influence. New forms were faddish froth: material the marrow. And what more arresting material than the self-revealing truth!

One important writer among the new Negroes stands out as having contributed nothing or little to this conglomeration. That writer is the poet Countee Cullen. He for himself (as well as others for him) has written numerous disclaimers of an attitude narrowed by racial influence. He may be right. Certainly *Caroling Dusk,* his anthology of "verse by Negro poets," represents a careful culling of the less distinctive, that is to say, the less Negroid poetry of his most defiantly Negro contemporaries. Nevertheless it remains that when writing on race material Mr. Cullen is at his best. His is an unfortunate attitude, for it has been deliberately acquired and in that sense is artificial, tending to create a kind of effete and bloodless poetry in the manner of Mr. Braithwaite. The essential quality of good poetry is utmost sincerity and earnestness of purpose. A poet untouched by his times, by his conditions, by his environment is only half a poet, for earnestness and sincerity grow in direct proportion as one feels intelligently the pressure of immediate life. One may not like the pressure and the necessities under which it forces one to labor, but one does not deny it. Donne, as he grew older, oppressed by the thought of his ultimate physical decay and the weight of his (often imaginary) sin, wrote of God and repentance. Aseeth with the romantic notions of the French revolution, Wordsworth elevated all of nature, including man, to a common kinship in the Divine. Now undoubtedly the biggest, single unalterable circumstance in the life of Mr. Cullen is his color. Most of the life he has lived has been influenced by it. And when he writes by it, he *writes;* but when this does not guide him, his pen trails faded ink across his pages.

To argue long about Countee Cullen—his ideas, his poetic creed, and the results he obtains—is to come face to face with the poet's own confusion. It is not a matter of words or language merely, as it was with Dunbar: it is a matter of ideas and feelings. Once Mr. Cullen wrote: "Negro verse (as a designation, that is) would be more confusing than accurate. Negro poetry, it seems to me, in the sense that we speak of Russian, French, or Chinese poetry, must emanate from some country other than this in some language other than our own."

At another time: "Somehow or other I find my poetry of itself treating of the Negro, of his joys and his sorrows—mostly of the latter—, and of the heights and depths of emotion which I feel as a Negro."

And at still another:

> Then call me traitor if you must,
> Shout treason and default!
> Saying I betray a sacred trust
> Aching beyond this vault.
> I'll bear your censure as your praise,
> For never shall the clan
> Confine my singing to its ways
> Beyond the ways of man.

The answer to all this seems to be: Chinese poetry translated into English remains Chinese poetry—Chinese in feeling, in ideas.

But there is no confusion in Mr. Cullen's first volume, *Color*, which is far and away his best. Here his poetry (nearly all of it on racial subjects, or definitely and frankly conditioned by race) helps to balance the savage poetic outbursts of Claude McKay. Countee Cullen is decidedly a gentle poet, a schoolroom poet whose vision of life is interestingly distorted by too much of the vicarious. This lends rather than detracts. It is as if he saw life through the eyes of a woman who is at once shrinking and bold, sweet and bitter. His province is the nuance, the finer shades of feeling, subtility and finesse of emotion and expression. Often however, with feline slyness, he bares the pointed talons of a coolly ironic and deliberate humor which is his way of expressing his resentment at the racial necessities.

> Once riding in old Baltimore,
> Heart-filled, head-filled with glee,
> I saw a Baltimorean
> Keep looking straight at me.

> Now I was eight and very small
>   And he was no whit bigger,
> And so I smiled, but he poked out
>   His tongue, and called me, "Nigger."
>
> I saw the whole of Baltimore
>   From May until December;
> Of all the things that happened there
>   That's all that I remember.

Again, in "To My Fairer Brethren":

> Though I score you with my best,
>   Treble circumstance
> Must confirm the verdict, lest
>   It be laid to chance.
>
> Insufficient that I match you
>   Every coin you flip;
> Your demand is that I catch you
>   Squarely on the hip.
>
> Should I wear my wreathes a bit
>   Rakishly and proud,
> I have bought my right to it;
>   Let it be allowed.

When he leaves work of this kind for the heavier moods and materials so popular with Hughes, McKay, Horne, Alexander, and *The
Crisis* and *Opportunity* poets, Mr. Cullen bogs down. He is the
Ariel of Negro poets. He cannot beat the tom-tom above a faint
whisper nor know the primitive delights of black rain and scarlet
sun. After the fashion of the years 1925–1928, he makes a return to
his African heritage, but not as a "son returned in bare time." He
was not among the Negroes who were made Africa conscious and
Africa proud by the striding Colossus, Marcus Garvey, by Vander-
cook's *Tom-Tom*, and O'Neill's *The Emperor Jones*. Cullen's gifts
are delicate, better suited to bons mots, epigrams, and the delight-
fully personal love lyrics for which a large circle admire him.

The title poem of his third volume, *The Black Christ*, illustrates
at once the scope and the limit of his abilities. Bitter and ironic in
its mood, revealing but slight narrative and dramatic powers, the
poem is feeble with the childish mysticism of a bad dream, pene-

trating the realm of emotional reality no more than does a child's relation of a nightmare. Here in this poem Mr. Cullen's lyricism is smothered, his metrical faults exaggerated, and his fear of stern reality italicized.

What did the new Negro have to say? What was he thinking? Truth to tell, he was becoming a first-class cynic with decidedly red tendencies. First of all, he deserted the church, that staunch bulwark of bourgeois conservatism, in great numbers. He started laughing at religion, and many began to use it merely as the tool of charlatanism. He lost rapidly all sense of ethical progression and, like his white contemporaries, acquired an exaggerated sense of the value of what he called economic stability. The Republican party became no longer the only party, for through defection to the Democrats the Negro passed on to Socialism, Communism, and even Nihilism. Though he laughed at the gaudy uniforms, jeered the unmanned and rotting ships of the Black Star Line, and derided the Utopian ideas of the leader of the Universal Negro Improvement Association, he was shocked by Marcus Garvey. He was shocked, alarmed, amazed at the gigantic demonstration of the herd instinct, and confused, confounded, and humiliated by the public disclosures of graft and incompetence. His illusions crashed about him. The hounds of inferiority bayed on his trail. He began to believe that but two ways were left open to him: the bitter indifference that begins the end, and escape—escape through conformity (possible only to the white-blacks), or through desertion of the "American way," or through absolute and unequivocal submission, or through atavistic reversion.

Most of this brooding thought was nourished by the work of certain white writers whose books have had a wide public since 1925. Certainly Julia Peterkin's *Black April* and *Scarlet Sister Mary,* with their return to old concepts and stereotypes (which she helped revive), did not further the Negro's self-respect. Dowd's pseudo-scientific *The American Negro* gave an air of authenticity to the utterances of the prejudiced southern press. The savage primitivism of DuBose Heyward's Porgy, Crown, and Bess, and of Eugene O'Neill's Brutus Jones seemed to indicate that the Negro was no more than a brute, while Carl Van Vechten's polite, light *Nigger Heaven* pictured him as absorbing all the vices and none of the virtues of white civilization.

In various guise the futility, the pessimism, the atavism began to appear in the literature of the new Negro. Langston Hughes might declare in extenuation, as he did in 1926, that the new Negro was bent upon writing what he wanted to write, that he stood, as it were, free on the mountaintop; but he did not mention that even there on the mountaintop he breathed the noxious air of desperation ascending from the valley. Not in joy but in desperation did the same poet write:

> Me an ma baby's
> Got two mo' ways,
> Two mo' ways to do de Charleston!
> > Da, da
> > Da, da, da!
> Two mo' ways to do de Charleston!
>
> Soft lights on the tables,
> Music gay,
> Brown-skin steppers
> In a cabaret.
>
> White folks, laugh!
> White folks, pray!
>
> Me an' ma baby's
> Got two mo' ways,
> Two mo' ways to do de Charleston!

Nor did he try to be brave and laughing with that bitter desperation of joy when he wrote:

> We cry among the skyscrapers
> As our ancestors
> Cried among the palms in Africa
> Because we are alone,
> It is night,
> And we're afraid.

Hughes is the most prolific and the most representative of the new Negroes. By training and experience he is at the opposite end from Cullen, that is to say, he is a Negro divinely capable of realizing (which is instinctive) and giving expression to (which is cultivated) the dark perturbation of the soul—there is no other word—of the Negro. There is this difference between racial thought and feeling: what the professors, the ministers, the physicians, the social workers think, the domestics, the porters, the dock hands, the factory girls, and the streetwalkers feel—feel in a great tide that pours over into song and shout, prayer and cursing, laughter and tears. More than any other writer of the race, Langston Hughes has been swept with this tide of feeling. This accounts for the fresh green of him, the great variety of his moods. "The tom-tom laughs, the tom-tom sobs," and between laugh and sob there is a scale of infinite distinctions.

But there is artifice, the cultivated, in him too. Certain of his pieces like "Cabaret" and "Saturday Night" quite evidently are tomfooleries as to form, but other pieces showing the strong influence of the midwestern poets are seriously experimental. Unless we consider as experiments the short stories of Frances Ellen Watkins and her retention of dialectal patterns without the dialect speech sounds, Negro writers had never experimented with form, and none since Dunbar had seriously tackled the problem of language. Mr. Hughes, more concerned with form than language, interested himself in a poetic design that would fit his material. The result is the Blues and the Shout. To the first he has given a strict poetic pattern; "one long line repeated, and a third line to rhyme with the first two. Sometimes the second line in repetition is slightly changed and sometimes, but very seldom, it is omitted." The Shout also has a pattern, definite but flexible. It takes its name from the single line of strophic and incremental significance which is shouted or moaned after each two, three, or four line stanza. There is also evidence that Mr. Hughes more recently has been experimenting with short story forms.

Mr. Hughes's experiments do not touch his more deeply moving verse. Is it that the bizarre forms, like the bizarre language of dialect, impose limitations upon expression? When he wishes to get beyond these, Mr. Hughes resorts to the purer verse forms as in "The Negro Speaks of Rivers," "Cross," and "I, Too." Certainly none of the Blues, no matter how full of misery, and none of the Shouts, no matter how full of religion, ever get beyond a certain scope of feeling. He can catch up the dark messages of Negro feeling and express them in what he calls "racial rhythms," but it is as the iteration of the drum rather than the exposition of the piano. He feels in them, but he does not think. And this is the source of his naïvete.

But Langston Hughes is not all naïvete either. His short stories are a case in point. The title story of his volume of stories, *The*

*Ways of White Folks,* and such stories as "Cora Unashamed" and
"Camp Meeting" are caviar to the general. Such stories as these map
the broad highways of indifference, of primitivism, of futility down
which the Negro artist is escaping to his end—or his beginning. The
beautiful black Cora, unadapted and unadaptable, was lost in the
complexities of a society of which she should have been a part. Mr.
Hughes, if you will, makes us see how undesirable such a society is,
but the fact remains that the individual must conform to society. It
is victory to live in Rome. Cora knew neither victory nor defeat—
simply nullification. And it is the same with the characters in the
novel *Not Without Laughter.* Aunt Hagar is as the door between
that world from which the Negro had struggled since slavery, the
world of poverty, of strife, of the inescapable consequences of being
black, and that other world of smug physical comforts, of middle-
class respectability into which her daughter Tempy had passed as
into heaven. But to the other daughters, Annjee and Harriet,
Tempy's world is no more satisfactory than their own. They do not
want these imitation worlds of white folks' making.


# II


What happened in Negro literature from the appearance of Van
Vechten's *Nigger Heaven* in 1926 until 1935 is obvious. First of all,
Negro writers, both poets and novelists, centered their attentions so
exclusively upon life in the great urban centers that the city, especially Harlem, became an obsession with them. Now Harlem life is
far from typical of Negro life; indeed, life there is lived on a
theatrical plane that is as far from true of Negro life elsewhere as
life in the Latin Quarter is from the truth of life in Picardy. The
Negro writers' mistake lay in the assumption that what they saw
was Negro life, when in reality it was just Harlem life. Very shortly,
for literary purposes anyway, Harlem became a sort of disease in the
American organism.

Again, it was not upon the New Yorker (as distinguished from the
Harlemite) that the Negro writers concentrated. Driven by the restless demons of their own forebodings, doubts, despairs, they sought
the food necessary to the appetites of these spiritual and intellectual
furies. The very things that caused their illness they fed upon. They

needed whores, pimps, the sweetmen; *bistros,* honky-tonks, spider-nests; the perverse, the perverted, the psychopathic. They found them, of course, in abundance. In this it might be said, somewhat in extenuation, that they seemed to follow fashion.

It is to this last—the following of fashion—that certain critics would affix all the blame for what it has pleased one of them to call "the degraded literature." But it was more than just fashion: the thing the new Negro followed was soul-deep. Popular writers follow the fashions in literature in order to make money. No one of the new Negroes can be accused of making money, or even of wanting to make money. Langston Hughes was undoubtedly right when he declared of the younger Negro artists: "If the white people are pleased, we are glad. If they are not, it doesn't matter. . . . If colored people are pleased, we are glad. If they are not, their displeasure doesn't matter either." It just happened that *Nigger Heaven* created a variation on a demand that the Negro writers were spiritually and psychologically prepared to fill. This literature would have been anyway. Some of it, as a matter of fact, had been written before *Nigger Heaven.* It is literature of escape. Literature of escape becomes necessary to a people in times of great moral and social stress. McKay and Hughes, Thurman and Larsen were no more immune to the catastrophic pressure of the war and the changes with which its aftermath affected their common lot than were Faulkner and Hemingway, Remarque and Sheriff safe from such pressure and the changes in their own lives. Negro mothers, too, bore children into the "lost generation."

There is something of wonder in the fact that a quiet little book of brilliant poems appearing in 1927 was not overlooked. The book was *God's Trombones: Seven Negro Sermons in Verse,* and its author was James Weldon Johnson. Like its foremost contemporaries (*Fine Clothes to the Jew* had appeared the same year and *Weary Blues* the year before), *God's Trombones,* too, made a return to the primitive heritage, but not in the sensational and superficial way of the younger writers. "The Creation" and "Go Down Death," two of the seven sermons, are among the most moving poems in the language and certainly rank with the best things done by American Negro poets. But it is not enough merely to say this, for it explains nothing of another significance.

In 1917 Mr. Johnson's first volume of poems, *Fifty Years,* was published. A section of this book was called "Croons and Jingles" out of consideration for the limitations of the dialect the author used in such pieces as "Sence You Went Away":

> Seems lak to me de stars don't shine so bright,
> Seems lak to me de sun done loss his light,
> Seems lak to me der's nothin' goin' right,
>     Sence you went away.

Under this section also Mr. Johnson made limited use of folk material. *The Book of American Negro Poetry* was issued in 1922. It was not nearly so definitive as the title implies, but Mr. Johnson's preface as editor indicates that he had given important thought to folk material and its mode of expression. In that scholarly essay he said: "What the colored poet in the United States needs to do is something like what Synge did for the Irish. . . . He needs a form that is freer and larger than dialect, but which will still hold the racial flavor; a form expressing the imagery, the idioms, the peculiar turns of thought and the distinctive humor and pathos, too, of the Negro, but which will also be capable of voicing the deepest and highest emotions and aspirations and allow of the widest range of subjects and the widest scope of treatment." This same preoccupation is also evident in Mr. Johnson's preface to *The Book of American Negro Spirituals.*

Then came *God's Trombones* as a brilliant example of the maturing of his thoughts on folk material and dialect. Aside from the beauty of the poems, the essay which prefaces them is of the first importance for it definitely hails back from the urban and sophisticated to the earthy exuberance of the Negro's kinship with the earth, the fields, the suns and rains of the South. Discarding the "mutilations of dialect," Mr. Johnson yet retains the speech forms, the idea patterns, and the rich racial flavor.

> O Lord, we come this morning
> Knee-bowed and body-bent
> Before thy throne of grace.

\*     \*     \*

> And now, O Lord—
> When I've done drunk my last cup of sorrow—
> When I've been called everything but a child of God—

When I'm done travelling up the rough side of the mountain—
O—Mary's Baby—
When I start down the steep and slippery steps of death—
When this old world begins to rock beneath my feet—
Lower me to my dusty grave in peace
To wait for that great gittin' up morning.

But more important still is Mr. Johnson's acknowledgment of his debt to the folk material, the primitive sermons, and the influence of the spirituals, for it is undoubtedly Mr. Johnson's return to these things that has influenced the gratifying new work of Sterling Brown in poetry and Zora Neale Hurston in prose. What Mr. Johnson has said of Sterling Brown in the preface to *Southern Road* might also be said (and Miss Fannie Hurst nearly says it) of Zora Hurston's *Jonah's Gourd Vine* and *Mules and Men*. Mr. Johnson said: "For his raw material he dug down into the deep mine of Negro folk poetry. He found the unfailing sources from which sprang the Negro folk epics and ballads such as 'Stagolee,' 'John Henry,' 'Casey Jones,' 'Long Gone John' and others. . . . He has made more than mere transcriptions of folk poetry, and he has done more than bring to it mere artistry; he has deepened its meaning and multiplied its implications."

To understand what Mr. Johnson means, to know how this new work differs from the old, one has only to read such things as "Southern Road," "When De Saints Go Marching Home," "Frankie and Johnny," and "Memphis Blues," quoted below:

I

Nineveh, Tyre,
Babylon,
Not much lef'
Of either one.
All dese cities
Ashes and rust,
De win' sing sperrichals
Through deir dus' . . .
Was another Memphis
Mongst de olden days,
Done been destroyed
In many ways . . .
Dis here Memphis

It may go;
Floods may drown it;
Tornado blow;
Mississippi wash it
Down to sea—
Like de other Memphis in
History.

## II

Watcha gonna do when Memphis on fire,
   Memphis on fire, Mistah Preachin' Man?
Gonna pray to Jesus and nebber tire,
    Gonna pray to Jesus, loud as I can,
      Gonna pray to my Jesus, oh, my Lawd!

Watcha gonna do in de hurricane,
   In de hurricane, Mistah Workin' Man?
Gonna put dem buildings up again,
    Gonna put em up dis time to stan',
      Gonna push a wicked wheelbarrow, oh, my Lawd!

Watcha gonna do when de flood roll fas',
   Flood roll fas', Mistah Gamblin' Man?
Gonna pick up my dice fo' one las' pass—
    Gonna fade my way to de lucky lan',
      Gonna throw my las' seven—oh, my Lawd!

## III

Memphis go
By Flood or Flame;
Nigger won't worry
All de same—
Memphis go
Memphis come back,
Ain't no skin
Off de nigger's back.
All dese cities
Ashes, rust. . . .
De win' sing sperrichals
Through deir dus'.

Certainly the first and second sections of *Southern Road* and the
tales in *Mules and Men* mean something. They mean a sweet return

In time, for though the sun is setting on
A song-lit race of slaves, it has not set;
Though late, O soil, it is not too late yet
To catch thy plaintive soul, leaving, soon gone,
Leaving, to catch thy plaintive soul soon gone.

It is this that must happen; a spiritual and physical return to the earth. For Negroes are yet an earthy people, a people earth-proud— the very salt of the earth. Their songs and stories have arisen from a loving bondage to the earth, and to it now they must return. It is to this, for pride, for strength, for endurance, that they must go back. Sterling Brown says it in "Strange Legacies":

Brother,
When, beneath the burning sun
The sweat poured down and breath came thick,
And the loaded hammer swung like a ton
And the heart grew sick;
You had what we need now, John Henry.
Help us get it.

# The Black Aesthetic
# in the Thirties, Forties, and Fifties

## by Dudley Randall

Every poet is molded by his age, by the great events or Great Event that took place during his impressionable years. In the thirties it was the Great Depression and the Spanish Civil War. In the forties it was World War II. In the fifties it was McCarthyism, the Korean War, and the beginning of the Freedom movement with the Supreme Court school-desegregation decision of 1954.

Some poets, such as Langston Hughes and Arna Bontemps, lived from the Negro Renaissance through the post-Renaissance period into the period of the Black Aesthetic and black power of the sixties. Others, like Gwendolyn Brooks and Robert Hayden, published their first books in the forties and are still creating. I shall describe these later poets only as they wrote in the middle period between the Renaissance and the Black Aesthetic, as their further development does not come within the scope of this essay.

During this middle period, and previously during the Harlem Renaissance, there was no such concept as a black aesthetic. Negro writers wanted to be accepted into the mainstream of American literature. The closest thing to a black aesthetic was Langston Hughes's declaration in "The Negro Artist and the Racial Mountain" (1926). He wrote:

> One of the most promising of the young Negro poets said to me once, "I want to be a poet—not a Negro poet," meaning, I believe, "I want to write like a white poet"; meaning subconsciously, "I would like to be a white poet"; meaning behind that, "I would like to be white."

"The Black Aesthetic in the Thirties, Forties, and Fifties," by Dudley Randall. From *The Black Aesthetic*, Addison Gayle, Jr., ed. (Garden City, N.Y.: Doubleday and Company, Inc., 1971), pp. 224–34. Reprinted by permission of the author.

And I was sorry the young man said that, for no great poet has ever been afraid of being himself. And I doubted then that, with his desire to run away spiritually from his race, this boy would ever be a great poet. But this is the mountain standing in the way of any true Negro art in America—this urge within the race toward whiteness, the desire to pour racial individuality into the mold of American standardization, and to be as little Negro and as much American as possible.

Hughes went on to state:

. . . But, to my mind, it is the duty of the younger Negro artist, if he accepts any duty at all from outsiders, to change through the force of his art that old whispering "I want to be white," hidden in the aspirations of his people, to "Why should I want to be white? I am a Negro —and beautiful!"

This is as close to the Black Aesthetic cry of "I'm black, and beautiful!" as it is possible to come.

Hughes continued:

So I am ashamed for the black poet who says, "I want to be a poet, not a Negro poet," as though his own racial world were not as interesting as any other world.

Hughes concluded with the oft-quoted declaration:

We younger Negro artists who create now intend to express our individual dark-skinned selves without fear or shame. If white people are pleased, we are glad. If they are not, it doesn't matter. We know we are beautiful. And ugly too. The tom-tom cries and the tom-tom laughs. If colored people are pleased we are glad. If they are not, their displeasure doesn't matter either. We build our temples for tomorrow, strong as we know how, and we stand on top of the mountain, free within ourselves.

This sounds much like the Black Aesthetic credo, but there are significant points of difference. For instance, Hughes uses the word Negro. Some Negro ideologues have forbidden Negroes to call Negroes Negroes. Hughes stresses individualism ("express our individual dark-skinned selves"). In the Black Aesthetic, individualism is frowned upon. Feedback from black people, or the mandates of self-appointed literary commissars, is supposed to guide the poet. But Hughes says, "If colored people are pleased we are glad. If they are not, their displeasure doesn't matter either." (Another expression of individualism.) Hughes says, "We know we are beautiful. And ugly too." In the Black Aesthetic, Negroes are always beautiful.

In my own opinion, this feedback usually comes from the most vocal group, ideologues or politicians, who are eager to use the persuasiveness of literature to seize or consolidate power for themselves. Politicians such as Stalin or Khrushchev have a certain low cunning, but they cannot grasp the complexity or paradoxes of life and literature, and they try to impose their own simple-mindedness and conformity upon them.

The Great Event of the 1920s was the Depression. In contrast to the affluent 1960s, poverty was everywhere. Millionaires as well as poor people lost everything. Everyone was in this catastrophe together. Eyes were turned toward Russia and communism, and the Communists were active in organizing rent strikes, labor unions, and campaigns for relief. Federal Writers' Projects were started, where black and white authors worked together. Even if black writers did not join the Communist Party, as did Richard Wright, they were sympathetic toward it and its policy of non-discrimination. Black writers did not give up their struggle for Negro rights, but regarded it as part of the struggle for the rights of man everywhere. A popular union organizing slogan was, "Black and white, unite and fight."

Robert Hayden wrote his *Speech,* in which he urged black and white workers to cooperate:

> I have seen the hand
> Holding the blowtorch
> To the dark, anguish-twisted body;
> I have seen the hand
> Giving the high-sign
> To fire on the white pickets;
> And it was the same hand,
> Brothers, listen to me,
> It was the same hand.

The horizons of poets were widened beyond their own Negro struggle to include world events. In his first book, *Heart-Shape in the Dust,* Hayden wrote of youths dying in the Spanish Civil War, in *Spring Campaign:*

> She wears a gas mask, fair Corinna does,
> And thinks of spring's first air raid while
> seeking spring's first rose.

In the same book (1940), he foretold the death of Adolf Hitler, in *Prophecy:*

> He fell with his mouth
> Crushing into the cold earth
> And lay unharming at last
> Under the falling leaves and the fog. . . .
>
> They returned to the ruined city
> And began to build again.

Hayden's second book, *A Ballad of Remembrance,* was not published until 1962, but in the meantime there were the brochures *The Lion and the Archer* (with Myron O'Higgins, 1948) and *Figure of Time* (1955), published in his own "Counterpoise Series." The surrealistic *A Ballad of Remembrance* is chilling with its whirling, glittering images and rhythms and its feeling of nightmare and irrationality. It captures the black experience, but filtered through the poet's sensitive subjectivity:

> Accommodate, muttered the Zulu king, throned
> like a copper toad in a glaucous poison jewel.
> Love, chimed the saints and the angels and the mermaids
> Hate, shrieked the gumetal priestess
> from her spiked bellcollar curved like a fleur-de-lys!
>
> As well have a talon as a finger, a muzzle
> as a mouth. As well have a hollow as a heart.
> And she pinwheeled away in coruscations
> of laughter, scattering those others before her.

In *Middle Passage* and *Runagate Runagate,* Hayden incorporates all the innovations of the experimental poets of the 1920s: varied and expressive rhythms; anti-poetic materials such as quotations from handbills, legal documents, ships' logs; scraps of poetry, hymns, spirituals; fusing all these together to make two exciting narratives of the beginning and of the escape from slavery.

Gwendolyn Brooks, in *A Street in Broneville* (1945), wrote of the black people on the South Side of Chicago, but world events widened her vision to include also sonnets of black men at war. In her Pulitzer prize-winning *Annie Allen* (1949), she uses many poetic forms with easy mastery, from ballads to crisp sonnets:

What shall I give my children? who are poor,
Who are adjudged the leastwise of the land,
Who are my sweetest lepers, who demand
No velvet and no velvety velour. . . .

In the tight, seven-lined trochaic stanzas of *The Anniad,* she deftly
balances narrative, images, and rhythm:

Leads her to a lonely room

Which she makes a chapel of.
Where she genuflects to love.
All the prayerbooks in her eyes
Open soft as sacrifice
Or the dolour of a dove.
Tender candles ray by ray
Warm and gratify the gray.

Like Tolson and Hayden, she has the long poem firmly in control.

Langston Hughes continued to write of black urban folk, but
now he abandoned the glamour of night clubs and of a Harlem
pandering to white seekers of thrills. He wrote of the maids, porters,
and laborers of Harlem instead of the dancers, singers, and "lean-
headed jazzers" of the cabarets. His series on "Madame Alberta K.
Washington" presents with humor a strong-minded Negro domestic
worker.

He still wrote on racial themes, but he wrote within the context
of democracy for all. The Negro struggle was a part of the world-
wide struggle for freedom. This universality is expressed in *I Dream
a World:*

A world I dream where black or white,
Whatever race you be,
Will share the bounties of the earth
And every man is free. . . .

In his poems, instances of injustice are ironically juxtaposed with
the American Dream or with American ideals, as in his poem *Freedom Train.* An unsolvable dilemma is presented in his *Merry-Go-
Round,* where a Negro child asks in frustration, where is the back of
the merry-go-round, as black people always have to sit at the back.

The very title of M. B. Tolson's book *Rendezvous with America*
(1944) suggests a widening of the poet's interest. He writes from the

point of view of the Negro, but he has expanding sympathy with other ethnic groups, shown in his title poem.

> A blind man said,
> "Look at the kikes,"
> And I saw
> Rosenwald sowing the seeds of culture in the Black Belt. . . .
>
> A blind man said,
> "Look at the Chinks,"
> And I saw
> Lin Yutang crying the World Charter in the white man's
> wilderness. . . .

In this book, Tolson uses a wide variety of poetic forms, from rhymed quatrains and sonnets to long poems written in varying measures. He shows his architectonic power in building long poems that do not bore the reader, foreshadowing his mastery of longer forms in *Libretto for the Republic of Liberia* and *Harlem Gallery*. His sonnets are dramatic—compressing narrative, characterization, theme, and dramatic tension into fourteen lines. Perhaps his most successful sonnet is *Incident at Versailles*, with its succinct characterization of Clemenceau, Lloyd George, and Wilson, and its implicit prophecy of all the future disasters that were to spring from the racism of these world leaders. In general, the language of the poems is vigorous, although it is sometimes marred by clichés and archaic syntax.

In 1953 he published *Libretto for the Republic of Liberia,* a long poem commissioned for the centennial of the African nation, which earned him the title of Poet Laureate of Liberia. The preface was written by Allen Tate, and appeared also in *Poetry* magazine, with an excerpt from the book.

In his preface, Tate said that Tolson had for the first time incorporated the modern poetic language into a poem written by a Negro. In this poem, Tolson used all the devices dear to the New Criticism: recondite allusions, scraps of foreign languages, African proverbs, symbolism, objective correlatives. Many parts of the poem are obscure, not through some private symbolism of the author, but because of the unusual words, foreign phrases, and learned allusions. If the reader has a well-stored mind, or is willing to use dictionaries, encyclopedias, atlases, and other reference books, the poem should present no great difficulty. Reading this poem is like reading other learned poets, such as Milton and T. S. Eliot.

The history of the poem is interesting. Tolson sent the manuscript to Tate, who returned it. Then Tolson rewrote the poem according to the tenets of the New Criticism. The irony is that, about this time, the New Criticism was declining, and the Beat poets, with their looser, freer, more emotional language and form, were coming into popularity. In any case, the learned allusive language is not the spontaneous speech of the Negro people.

Hayden, Brooks, and Tolson can be grouped together as poets conscious of technique, who were familiar with and learned from the modern experimental masters such as Hart Crane, Eliot, Pound, and Yeats, and not from minor poets such as Housman or Edna St. Vincent Millay, or traditional poets such as Keats, all of whom influenced Countee Cullen.

They were conscious of their Negro race, but they regarded it in the wider context of a world-wide depression and a world-wide war against fascism. Their world view was wider and more inclusive than that of the Renaissance poets.

Other poets, perhaps not more conscious of race, but in whose work race occupies a more central position, were Sterling Brown, Margaret Walker, and Frank Marshall Davis.

Sterling Brown was in the same age group as the Renaissance poets, but his sole collection of poetry, *Southern Road,* was published in 1932. In this book, the influence of Negro folk poetry, of spirituals, blues, and ballads, is evident. Like Langston Hughes, he brings the blues stanza into formal verse. He has the unusual and valuable quality of humor, which permeates his ballads of Slim Greer, a picaresque adventurer. There are ballads of John Henry and of the chain gang, and poems of sharecroppers and southern rural life. These are poems of Negro life written out of black experience grounded in folk poetry which he intensifies with his art.

Margaret Walker, born in Jackson, Mississippi, is also influenced by Negro folk poetry. In her only volume of poetry, *For My People,* published in 1942 in the Yale University Series of Younger Poets, there are ballads of rural southern folk, of the witch Molly Means, of "Bad-man Stagolee" and "Big John Henry."

Unlike Brown, however, whose poems not in the folk tradition and folk forms were apt to be personal and subjective, Walker used the classical sonnet form (sometimes without rhyme) to write about Negroes. The sonnet about miners and sharecroppers titled *Childhood*, and the one titled *The Struggle Staggers Us* are outstanding in this series.

> Ours is a struggle from a too-warm bed;
> too cluttered with a patience full of sleep.
> Out of this blackness we must struggle forth;
> from want of bread, of pride, of dignity.

More experimental than Brown, and probably influenced by Carl Sandburg, she wrote some poems in long free-verse paragraphs like those of Fenton Johnson. The most famous of these is the title poem, *For My People*. This poem gains its force not by tropes—turns of language or thought—or logical development of a theme, but by the sheer overpowering accumulation of a mass of details delivered in rhythmical parallel phrases. *We Have Been Believers* is another powerful poem in a similar form and on a racial theme.

Race is central also in Frank Marshall Davis' books *Black Man's Verse, I Am the American Negro,* and *47th Street.*

A Chicago poet, he is inspired not by traditional Negro folk poetry, as are Brown and Walker, but by the teeming black life of a northern metropolis. His free verse shows the influence of Sandburg and Masters. In *Giles Johnson Ph.D.* and *Robert Whitmore,* he satirizes the pretensions of the black bourgeoisie. In the labor-organizing thirties, he wrote of sharecroppers and labor unions. His poetry is black-centered, without the focus on wider horizons found in the poetry of Hayden and Tolson.

Fenton Johnson was another poet who wrote in free verse influenced by Carl Sandburg. His earlier poetry was romantic, conventional, and traditional. In his later poetry he adopted the long free-verse line-strophe of Sandburg, and wrote poems expressing his disillusionment with America. Although marred by clichés and conventional expressions such as "fallen woman," they are new and different in their mood of frustration and despair.

These poets exemplify the trends of the thirties, forties, and fifties. There was a world depression, and a world war. In their outlook, black poets saw race as one problem among the world problems of poverty and fascism, and appealed to all men of good will to help solve the problem. As for their style, they no longer considered it sufficient to pour new wine of content into old bottles of form, but absorbed the techniques of the experimental poets Hart Crane, Pound, and Eliot. In this group were Tolson, Hayden, and Brooks. Another group—Brown, Walker, Davis, and Fenton Johnson—were influenced in varying degrees by Negro folk poetry and by Sandburg and Masters. Race was central in their poetry. Langston Hughes, growing beyond the Renaissance attraction to the more superficial and merely picturesque aspects of Negro life, wrote of its more serious aspects in the speech of the urban working man and in blues and jazz cadences.

There was no consciously formulated Black Aesthetic. Black poets considered themselves as part of American literature, although most of them were excluded from textbooks, anthologies, and, to a great extent, from magazines. It remains to be seen whether, in our time, the Black Aesthetic will stimulate superior poetry. The proof will have to be in the poems produced.

However, I will not hedge in caution, but will be imprudent enough to weigh the historical facts, note the trends, and make a prediction.

In the forties, black poets absorbed the innovations of white poets. In future years, they will not only absorb them, but will transcend them, and create their own innovations. Both Don Lee and Ameer Baraka are well-read, but they and poets like them will not only absorb what they've read, but, using their heritage of folk poetry and black music, will build something new upon that. In short, they'll do their own thing. They will not depend upon white publishers, white audiences, or white critics, as there are black publishers, black critics, and an increasing black audience. Robert Hayden and Gwendolyn Brooks are mature and at the height of their powers, and are capable of change and growth. There are many younger poets not yet even published in book form. All that I can foresee is a poetry of increasing power and richness, which will make a glorious contribution to the world.

# The Good Black Poet
## and the Good Gray Poet:
## The Poetry of Hughes and Whitman[1]

### *by Donald B. Gibson*

A direct link between Langston Hughes and Walt Whitman is
established by Hughes himself in a tribute to the poet, called "Old
Walt."[2]

> Old Walt Whitman
> Went finding and seeking,
> Finding less than sought
> Seeking more than found,
> Every detail minding
> Of the seeking or the finding.
>
> Pleasured equally
> In seeking as in finding,
> Each detail minding,
> Old Walt went seeking
> And finding.

"The Good Black Poet and the Good Gray Poet: The Poetry of Hughes and
Whitman," by Donald B. Gibson. From *Langston Hughes: Black Genius*, Therman B. O'Daniel, ed. (New York: William Morrow & Company, Inc., 1971), pp.
65–80. Reprinted by permission of the publisher.

[1] My initial thoughts about this subject appear in the introduction to *Five
Black Writers: Essays on Wright, Ellison, Baldwin, Hughes, and LeRoi Jones*,
Donald B. Gibson, ed. (New York: New York University Press, 1970).

[2] *Selected Poems of Langston Hughes* (New York: Alfred A. Knopf, 1959),
p. 100. The notion expressed in the poem of the poet as seeker is of course
traditional. Emerson said, "I am an endless seeker with no past at my back."
The specific idea of Whitman as seeker might have come from "Facing West
from California's Shores" whose second line reads, "Inquiring, tireless, seeking
what is yet unfound . . ."

If we were to substitute "Old Lang" for "Old Walt" throughout, we would have a poem as applicable to the one poet as to the other. The easiness of such a substitution is a clue to the relation between the two poets. The meaning of Hughes's poem is in its tone, its spirit, rather than its concreteness and specificity. It conveys an attitude rather than precise meaning. The relation between the two consists in their sharing common attitudes, certain feelings about what is worthwhile and valuable. Hughes, then, is not a direct descendant of Whitman; he was probably more directly influenced by Carl Sandburg and Vachel Lindsay and hence in regard to influence is at one remove. And in some very important ways Hughes is even much unlike Whitman—the comparison I am making should not obscure this fact. Yet, had Whitman not written, Hughes could not have been the same poet.

The two poets reveal in their poems certain rather obvious similarities. Hughes and Whitman are firm believers in the possibilities of realizing the American ideal. Both see the American nation in the process of becoming. Both are more cheerful than not. Both approached the writing of their poems in generally nontraditional fashion, though Hughes employs rhyme and traditional metrics more so than Whitman. Both are free in their choice of subject, writing about matters (especially sexual matters) traditionally considered unsuitable for poetry. Both adopt personae, preferring to speak in voices other than their own. They are social poets in the sense that they rarely write about private, subjective matters, about the workings of the inner recesses of their own minds.[3] Finally, they have a remarkably similar notion of the nature and function of poetry. Let us now examine these likenesses in greater detail.

Whitman and Hughes are democrats to the bone. Whitman's firm commitment to democracy and to the United States is well enough known.[4] He is most commonly known as the poet of American democracy, and his most widely known works have been such poems as "I Hear America Singing," "For You O Democracy," "O Captain! My Captain!" and others which reflect in various ways his commitment to democracy. Convinced of the essential unity of man-

---

[3] Hughes thought of himself as a social poet. One of his essays is titled "My Adventures as a Social Poet," *Phylon*, VIII (Third Quarter, 1947), 205–212.

[4] See "Democracy" in Roger Asselineau's brilliant *The Evolution of Walt Whitman: The Creation of a Personality*, 2 vols. [Translated by Richard P. Adams and the author] (Cambridge: Harvard University Press, 1960–1962), II.

kind, Whitman found democracy so appealing because of its promise to do away with social distinctions. Democracy was compatible with Whitman's philosophical notions about the ultimate unity of all things. Indeed the thrust of a good deal of his poetry is toward the doing away with distinctions between things.

Hughes also wanted to break down distinctions. His desire to break down the kinds of distinctions which make racism possible is not unrelated to a yearning to break down distinctions of all kinds. His "I, Too," "Low To High," and "High To Low," "In Explanation of Our Times," "Freedom's Plow," and "Democracy" all express Hughes's desire to see unity among people and a social, economic, and cultural equality among the peoples not only of America, but of the world. The forms of many of his poems indicate his desire to break down the traditionally rigid distinctions between poetry and prose.[5] Though he did not go as far as Whitman in his desire to see all things as related, his tendencies were in that direction. He valued flexibility and abhorred rigidity. His temperament was such that he was much more inclined to see the unity of experience than its disparity. Hence the title of one of his books of short stories, *Something in Common.*

Rather than relate to any developed (or at least publically stated) philosophical perspective—as Whitman's desire to do away with distinctions does—Hughes's proclivities in this direction seem to be most easily explained by reference to personality. *The Big Sea* and *I Wonder as I Wander* reveal a man of large sympathies, at ease in the world, broad in outlook, and fantastically regardful of other people. One would expect that he would be as strongly antifascistic as he is and as indifferent to puritanical moral values even if his autobiographical writings and poetry did not make it so clear. He seems antiauthoritarian by nature, democratic by virtue of character. His politics are as natural to him as breathing.

Hughes's commitment to the American ideal was deep felt and abiding. He held on to it despite his acute awareness of the inequities of democracy, and he seemed to feel that in time justice would prevail, that the promises of the dream would be fulfilled. His early poem "I, Too" (*The Weary Blues*, 1926)[6] is testimony to his faith.

---

[5] Whitman wanted to break down the distinction too. See F. O. Matthiessen, *American Renaissance* (New York: Oxford University Press, 1941), p. 580.

[6] *Selected Poems*, p. 275.

I, too, sing America.

I am the darker brother.
They send me to eat in the kitchen
When company comes,
But I laugh,
And eat well,
And grow strong.

Tomorrow,
I'll be at the table
When company comes.
Nobody'll dare
Say to me,
"Eat in the kitchen,"
Then.

The later long poem "Freedom's Plow," [7] written during World War
II and having about it something of a patriotic, wartime flair, is no
less an expression of the poet's basic feeling.

America!
Land created in common,
Dream nourished in common,
Keep your hand on the plow! Hold on!
If the house is not yet finished,
Don't be discouraged, builder!
If the fight is not yet won,
Don't be weary, soldier!
The plan and pattern is here,
Woven from the beginning
Into the warp and woof of America . . .

In an essay titled "My America" Hughes attempted to express his
complex feelings about the United States. The essay begins "This is
my land America. Naturally, I love it—it is home—and I am vitally
concerned about its mores, its democracy, and its well-being." The
piece concludes with another testament of faith: ". . . we know
. . . that America is a land in transition. And we know it is within
our [black people's] power to help in its further change toward a
finer and better democracy than any citizen has known before. The
American Negro believes in democracy. We want to make it real,

[7] *Ibid.*, pp. 291–297. Quoted lines from p. 296.

complete, workable, not only for ourselves—the fifteen million dark ones—but for all Americans all over the land." [8]

As optimists generally do, Langston Hughes and Walt Whitman lacked a sense of evil. This (and all it implies) puts Hughes in a tradition with other American writers. He stands with Whitman, Emerson, Thoreau, and later with Sandburg, Lindsay, and Steinbeck, as opposed to Hawthorne, Poe, Melville, James, Faulkner, and Eliot. This is not to say that he did not recognize the existence of evil, but, as Yeats says of Emerson and Whitman, he lacked the "Vision of Evil." He did not see evil as inherent in the character of nature and man, and hence he felt that the evil (small "e") about which he wrote so frequently in his poems (lynchings, segregation, discrimination of all kinds) would be eradicated with the passage of time. Of course the Hughes of *The Panther and the Lash* (1967) is not as easily optimistic as the poet was twenty or twenty-five years before. Hughes could not have written "I, Too" or even "The Negro Speaks of Rivers" in the sixties. But the evidence as I see it demonstrates that though he does not speak so readily about the fulfillment of the American ideal for black people, and though something of the spirit of having waited too long prevails, still the optimism remains. This is evidenced by his choosing to include the poems with an optimistic bias in his last two volumes of verse, *Selected Poems* and *The Panther and the Lash*.

*Montage of a Dream Deferred* (1951), included in *Selected Poems,* describes the dream as deferred, not dead or incapable of fulfillment. There is a certain grimness in the poem—for example in its most famous section, "Harlem," which begins, "What happens to a dream deferred? / Does it dry up / like a raisin in the sun?" But the grimness is by no means unrelieved. There is, in fact, a lightness of tone throughout the poem which could not exist did the poet see the ravages of racial discrimination as manifestations of Evil.

> On the day when the Savoy
> leaps clean over to Seventh Avenue
> and starts jitterbugging
> with the Renaissance,
> on that day when Abyssinia Baptist Church

---

[8] *The Langston Hughes Reader* (New York: George Braziller, Inc., 1958), pp. 500–501.

[9] Matthiessen, *American Renaissance*, p. 181.

throws her enormous arms around
St. James Presbyterian . . .[10]

\*    \*    \*

Maybe it ain't right—
but the people of the night
    will give even
    a snake
    a break.[11]

The whole tone of *Montage of a Dream Deferred* is characterized by
the well-known "Ballad of the Landlord." There the bitter-sweet
quality of Hughes's attitude toward his subject is clear.

*The Panther and the Lash* is the least cheerful, the least optimistic
of Hughes's volumes of poetry. Even this book, however, is not de-
void of hope.

Quick, sunrise, come!
Sunrise out of Africa,
Quick, come!
Sunrise, please come!
Come! Come![12]

\*    \*    \*

Four little girls
Might be awakened someday soon
By songs upon the breeze
As yet unfelt among magnolia trees.[13]

\*    \*    \*

In some lands
Dark night
And cold steel
Prevail—
But the dream
Will come back,
And the song

[10] *Selected Poems*, p. 240.

[11] *Ibid.*, p. 242.

[12] Langston Hughes, *The Panther and the Lash* (New York: Alfred A. Knopf,
1967), p. 13.

[13] *Ibid.*, p. 47.

Break
Its jail.[14]

\*       \*       \*

The past has been a mint
Of blood and sorrow.
That must not be
True of tomorrow.[15]

It must be said in all truth that though Hughes's optimism remains, his faith is not so much in democracy, nor in America, nor, for that matter in any specifically stated program or system. *The Panther and the Lash* reveals a generalized hope and optimism very much dimmed, comparatively. There is in respect to optimism no poem the least bit like "I, Too."

Whitman and Hughes share a similar attitude toward the relation of the poet to poetic tradition. Neither looked to the past for the sake of discovering suitable or acceptable forms or subject matter. Both poets were thoroughly engaged in their time, and were primarily men of the present and the future. I say "primarily" because both used to some extent the methods of traditional poetry—rhyme, regular metrical structures, poetic diction. But their work gives the impression on the whole that they were more reliant on their own sense of what constitutes poetry, were more inclined to look inward than outward in creating poems. Both found free verse to be more compatible with their aims than more structured verse, though Hughes probably relied more so than did Whitman on traditional form. Whitman, of course, is our most original poet even though he was influenced by others. Hughes looked to other poets, but to his contemporaries:

> Ethel Weimer [a high school English teacher] discovered Carl Sandburg for me. Although I had read of Carl Sandburg before . . . I didn't really know him until Miss Weimer in second-year English brought him, as well as Amy Lowell, Vachel Lindsay, and Edgar Lee Masters, to us. Then I began to try to write like Carl Sandburg.[16]

[14] *Ibid.,* p. 63.
[15] *Ibid.,* p. 69.
[16] Langston Hughes, *The Big Sea* (New York: Alfred A. Knopf, 1940), p. 28. This is an extremely important passage in this context, for it suggests that Hughes was probably more influenced by Whitman's follower, Sandburg, than by Whitman himself. Hughes's introduction to Whitman must have come later.

Whitman and Hughes were as unconventional in their subject matter as in their form, and both were attacked for their lack of delicacy, especially in matters related to sex. An anonymous reviewer of the 1855 and 1856 editions of *Leaves of Grass* wrote in *The Christian Examiner,* "The book might pass for merely hectoring and ludicrous, if it were not something a great deal more offensive. We are bound in conscience to call it impious and obscene." [17] Hughes's *Fine Clothers to the Jew* was called "trash" by *The Pittsburgh Courier* in 1927. In a defense of his poems, published in the same newspaper, he wrote the following:

> My poems are indelicate. But so is life.
> I write about "harlots and gin-bibers." But they are human. Solomon, Homer, Shakespeare, and Walt Whitman were not afraid or ashamed to include them.[18]

Such attitudes as this are not inconsistent with the poets' general stance against the status quo. Both seek change in the American society, and both welcome change. Hence they are less bound than many others to institutionalized ways of perceiving and responding. "A Woman Waits for Me" must have been even more shocking to genteel readers in the nineteenth century than Hughes's "indelicacies" have been in the twentieth. But the salient point is that the two poets shared the same impulse: to write honestly and truly about what they saw around them, and not to allow considerations of propriety to obfuscate their vision.

Another similarity between them is their choosing to speak through a mask, a persona, Whitman more consistently than Hughes. The observation that the poet who speaks in *Leaves of Grass* and Walt Whitman the man are not one and the same is by now common knowledge. Stovall speaks of Whitman's "hero-poet" and warns us to avoid the temptation to identify the speaker of the poem with the historical personage.[19] Whitman's reasons for projecting into the poem a kind of mythical, larger-than-life hero are multifarious, but clearly enough he wished to convey the impression of a figure

[17] Reprinted in *Whitman the Poet*, John C. Broderick, ed. (Belmont, California: Wadsworth Publishing Company, 1962), p. 69.

[18] Reprinted in James A. Emanuel, *Langston Hughes* (New York: Twayne Publishers, 1967), p. 70.

[19] Floyd Stovall, "Walt Whitman and the American Tradition," *Virginia Quarterly Review*, XXXI (Autumn, 1955), 552.

who in spirit would contain the essence of the American nation and, ultimately, of humankind. Hughes's use of the persona is somewhat different though not always entirely dissimilar. The speaker, for example, of "I, Too" is obviously not an individual; his is a collective "I," the same representative figure who says, "I've known rivers" in "The Negro Speaks of Rivers." [20] Whereas Whitman's persona is a single, fairly consistent, developing consciousness, Hughes assumes a multitude of personae. At one time he is the spirit of the race who represents the Negro or Black Man. Then he is a shoeshine boy, a black mother, a black woman quarrelling with her husband, a black man without a job or money, a prostitute, a ghetto tenant. Sometimes he is a consciousness whose role is incapable of determination. And sometimes he speaks, though comparatively rarely, as the poet.

In those poems about black life, thought, and character we could say that the persona is the same. It may well be that we are expected to see a commonality among the various experiences set forth in Hughes's poems of this type. If so, then we could say that a consistent persona speaks in a great number of Hughes's poems.

Most of the poems of Hughes and Whitman have an end beyond themselves, and they differ, therefore, from the poetry of those who seek to write poems beautiful in themselves but void of ideas. In writing poetry Hughes and Whitman felt they were performing a function beyond mere entertainment. Both intended to influence the thinking and actions of men; both intended to change the world through their poetry. Whitman's output is suffused with poems whose intention is to instill in men's minds the basic tenets of democracy. Asselineau tells us that "the two democratic principles which Whitman proclaimed with the greatest enthusiasm as early as 1855 were Liberty and Equality." [21] Hughes likewise wished to encourage men to know and love democracy. One of many such poems about democracy and the value of freedom and equality is Hughes's "I Dream a World."

> I dream a world where all
> Will know sweet freedom's way,
> Where greed no longer saps the soul
> Nor avarice blights our day.

[20] Donald C. Dickinson, *A Bio-bibliography of Langston Hughes* (Hamden, Connecticut: Archon Books, 1967), p. 15.
[21] *The Evolution of Walt Whitman*, II, p. 149.

> A world I dream where black or white,
> Whatever race you be,
> Will share the bounties of the earth
> And every man is free . . .[22]

Both had a pretty clear idea of what the function of poetry should be, and though both wrote some poems whose character is not in accordance with that notion, the large majority of their poems indicates a rather basic consistency between their ideas of the function of poetry and the poems they actually wrote.

Just as Emerson's ideas of what a poet should be (set forth in his essay, "The Poet," and published eleven years before the first edition of *Leaves of Grass*) seem uncannily to describe Whitman, so Whitman's statements about how poetry should be written seem to codify Hughes's ideas and practice. In the preface to *November Boughs* Whitman says, "No one will get at my verses who insists upon viewing them as a literary performance, or attempt at such performance, or as aiming mainly toward art or aestheticism." [23] Clearly the same could be said about Hughes's verses. Likewise Whitman's following statements about the composition of verse describe, essentially, what were Hughes's practices.

Rules for Composition—A perfectly transparent plate-glassy style, artless, with no ornaments or attempts at ornaments, for their own sake . . .
Clearness, simplicity, no twistified or foggy sentences, at all—the most translucid clearness without variation.
Common idioms and phrases—Yankeeisms and vulgarisms—cant expressions, when very pat only.[24]

Hughes would have agreed with the sentiments expressed by Whitman in one of his conversations with Horace Traubel in regard to the nature of poetry.

He [Whitman] continued: "The trouble is that writers are too literary—too damned literary. There has grown up—Swinburne I think an apostle of it—the doctrine (you have heard of it? It is dinned everywhere), art for art's sake: think of it—art for art's sake. Let a man really accept that . . . and he is lost. . . . Instead of regarding litera-

---

[22] *Troubled Island,* An Opera in Three Acts, by William Grant Still; Libretto by Langston Hughes (New York: Leads Music Corporation, 1949), p. 15.
[23] Quoted from *Whitman the Poet,* p. 15.
[24] *Ibid.,* p. 55.

ture as only a weapon, an instrument, in the service of something larger than itself, it looks upon itself as an end—as a fact to be finally worshipped, adored. To me that's all a horrible blasphemy—a bad smelling apostasy." [25]

Such areas of agreement as these are not incidental—they imply a whole orientation. We need simply compare Langston Hughes's poem on Walt Whitman ("Old Walt") with Ezra Pound's "A Pact."

> I make a pact with you, Walt Whitman—
> I have detested you long enough.
> I come to you as a grown child
> Who has had a pig-headed father;
> I am old enough now to make friends.
> It was you that broke the new wood,
> Now is a time for carving.
> We have one sap and one root—
> Let there be commerce between us.[26]

The strong negativism of the tone of Pound's poem has at base nothing to do with judgment of poetic value. What Pound objects to is Whitman's orientation. He cannot abide that largeness of spirit, that breaking of the wood, that standing in opposition to tradition. The key lines in this poem are the sixth and seventh—"It was you that broke the new wood, / Now is a time for carving." "Breaking new wood" means going against tradition, seeking out new territory, writing lines which critics declare are not poetry. "Now is a time for carving" is at best condescension. The final lines of the poem about "one sap and one root" grudgingly admit that the kind of poetry Whitman writes is at least poetry. Hence the poem admits that all poetry is not "pure" poetry. At the same time it says that the *best* poetry is of a certain kind. Whitman wrote crude poetry, and what he did needs refinement. Hence Pound speaks to Whitman as an inferior, as one *worthy* of detestation, though not entirely. He does not consider the possibility that Walt Whitman may not even *want* to make a pact with him. Central to the difference Pound elucidates is the difference between the two poets' politics. Pound's sympathies lay with authoritarianism and Whitman's with democracy. The two perspectives produce completely different poets. Hughes wrote the

[25] *Ibid.*, p. 63.
[26] *Selected Poems of Ezra Pound* (New York: New Directions, 1957), p. 27.

kind of poetry that Walt Whitman wrote; he, therefore, could write an unambivalent poem in praise of Whitman. No poet so inclined toward authoritarianism could write such a poem. The authoritarian, dictatorial perspective is by definition opposed to Whitman's. The literary values of Hughes and Whitman stand in marked contrast not only to Pound's, but also to those of all writers who see literary art as being an end in itself. Writers such as Henry James and Eliot, writers who are aristocratic in orientation and authoritarian in their politics, naturally scorn the comparatively free styles and, indeed, the whole world view of a Whitman and a Hughes.

There are undoubtedly more parallels than I have pointed out between Whitman and Hughes, but it should also be noted that there are many, many differences as well. For one thing Hughes was not a mystic, nor does his poetry indicate any kind of supernatural belief.[27] He was a naturalist and a humanist, and his attention was toward this world. This seems to me to relate to Hughes's little poem "Personal."

> In an envelope marked:
> *Personal*
> God addressed me a letter.
> In an envelope marked:
> *Personal*
> I have given my answer.[28]

The poem, written by a naturalist, a disbeliever, is ironic, and the irony and mild humor consists in the fact that the poet equates himself with God and tells Him, man to man, what he thinks of Him.

Much of his poetry, unlike Whitman's, was written to be read aloud. Hughes must have read to more people than any other twentieth-century poet. Some of his most apparently mundane and lifeless poems sparkled to life in his reading of them. Unlike Whitman's, many of his poems depend upon the reader's specialized knowledge of his language—in this case, a colloquial black language, both urban and rural. Some readers simply cannot respond to much of his poetry because they do not know the rhythms, pronunciations, and meaning of his language. In this regard, although Whitman often forced the language to his own purposes, Hughes is

[27] Emanuel, *Langston Hughes*, p. 95.
[28] *Selected Poems of Langston Hughes*, p. 88.

the less formal poet. (Of course these observations do not apply to Hughes's more formal poems, which are usually quite conventional.)

Though Hughes was a great admirer of Whitman,[29] it is doubtful that he knew how Whitman the man really felt about black people. Asselineau points out in detail Whitman's strong personal aversion to black people.[30] His publisher in 1860, Eldridge, says of Whitman's views:

> Of the Negro race he had a poor opinion. He said that there was in the constitution of the Negro's mind an irredeemable trifling or volatile element, and that he would never amount to much in the scale of civilization. I never knew him to have a friend among the Negroes while he was in Washington, and he never seemed to care for them. . . . In defence of the Negro's capabilities I once cited to him Wendell Phillips' eloquent portrait of Toussaint L'Ouverture, the pure black Haytian warrior and statesman. . . . He thought it a fancy picture much overdrawn, and added humorously, paraphrasing Betsy Prig in "Martin Chuzzlewit," "I don't believe there was no such nigger." [31]

Asselineau reports that Whitman found it "curious to see Lincoln 'standing with his hat off' to a regiment of black troops 'just the same as the rest' as they passed by" [32] and that Whitman "in 1872, in the course of a visit to his sister's home in Vermont, rejoiced at not seeing a single Negro." [33] Asselineau also points out that Whitman all his life "continued to behave and react like a Long Island peasant whose grandparents had owned slaves." [34]

These feelings were for the most part personally expressed and did not enter directly into *Leaves of Grass*. On the contrary Whitman must have recognized the grave contradiction between his personal feelings and his notions about liberty and equality, and certainly did not wish the poet of the poems to appear to be a bigot. There is, however, no poem on the Emancipation Proclamation and only one

---

[29] Dickinson, p. 15.

[30] "Democracy and Racialism—Slavery," *The Evolution of Walt Whitman*, II, p. 179ff. I urge the reader to see this unusually sensitive treatment of the subject. Few, if any, white Americans could have written such a chapter. Asselineau sees subtleties that Whitman's critics have either failed to see or not bothered to see.

[31] *Ibid.*, p. 188.

[32] *Ibid.*, p. 190.

[33] *Ibid.*

[34] *Ibid.*, pp. 190–191.

allusion to emancipation in *Leaves of Grass*.[35] It should be pointed
out, in all fairness, that Whitman was not *simply* a bigot. He abhorred the fugitive slave law;[36] he felt slavery to be degrading to
slave and slave owner;[37] and he several times depicts the horrors of
slavery in *Leaves of Grass*. It is this latter aspect of Whitman's
character which Hughes knew from *Leaves of Grass* and admired.
Hence Hughes might have felt the same (or similarly) toward Whitman had he known of the good gray poet's personal repugnance
toward black people. Walt Whitman the man might have been a
bigot, but Walt Whitman the poet was a thoroughgoing equali-
tarian.

There are many more differences that might be pointed out. But
suffice it to say that in Whitman the poet, Hughes found a compatible spirit, a man of large sympathy, of broad vision, and great faith
in the potential of America and Americans. Hughes and Whitman
would have disagreed on many things had they known and talked
with each other, but on matters basic to the sustaining of life, on
matters having to do with the well-being of the majority of people,
they would have found many points of agreement. And it is for this
reason, it seems to me, that the two poets want comparison.

[35] *Ibid.*, p. 188.
[36] *Ibid.*, p. 187.
[37] *Ibid.*, p. 185.

# Christ in Alabama:
# Religion in the Poetry of Langston Hughes

*by James A. Emanuel*

Religion, because of its historical importance during and after slavery, is an undeniably useful theme in the work of any major Black writer. In a writer whose special province for almost forty-five years was more recent Black experience, the theme is doubly vital. Hughes's personal religious orientation is pertinent. Asked about it by the Reverend Dana F. Kennedy of the "Viewpoint" radio and television show (on December 10, 1960), the poet responded:

> I grew up in a not very religious family, but I had a foster aunt who saw that I went to church and Sunday school . . . and I was very much moved, always, by the, shall I say, the rhythms of the Negro church, . . . of the spirituals, . . . of those wonderful old-time sermons. . . . There's great beauty in the mysticism of much religious writing, and great help there—but I also think that we live in a world . . . of solid earth and vegetables and a need for jobs and a need for housing. . . .

Two years earlier, the poet had told John Kirkwood of British Columbia's *Vancouver Sun* (December 3, 1958): "I'm not anti-Christian. I'm not against anyone's religion. Religion is one of the innate needs of mankind. What I am against is the misuse of religion. But I won't ridicule it. . . . Whatever part of God is in anybody is not to be played with, and everybody has got a part of God in them."

These typical public protestations by Hughes boil down to his insistence that religion is naturally sacred and beautiful, and that its needful sustenance must not be exploited. This melding of sincere respect and guarded cynicism generally squares with present attitudes in Black communities. The question for critics is twofold: (1) What religious references, by category and in detail, are discernible in Hughes's poetry? and (2) To what degree has he given his religious observations and feelings enduring artistic form? The answer, which should be stricter than the following remarks, contributes to our understanding of what religion has done, and failed to do, for Black men.

Sixty-odd poems by Hughes (about seven percent of his total production) contain religious references, some rather slight or indirect. The simplest are found in a group of six lyrics and songs, composed variously between 1926 and 1964, that celebrate the story of the Christ Child. Two others humanize Jesus, "To Artina" (1959) and "Ma Lord" (1927).[1] The former does so only metaphorically; in it a lover speaks with almost threatening possessiveness to his beloved, affecting what he feels is a Godlike prerogative. The latter, which has connections with Hughes's short story "On the Road," is closely representative of the author's positive approach to religion. "Ma Lord," the poet explained on the program "Viewpoint," was inspired by a quaintly dressed old lady whom he saw in church when he was a boy in Lawrence, Kansas. Her reprimand to some youngsters giggling at her clung to the author's memory and grew into the poem. The first two stanzas read:

> Ma Lord ain't no stuck-up man.
> Ma Lord he ain't proud.
> When he goes a-walkin'
> He gives me his hand.
> "You ma friend," he 'lowed.
>
> Ma Lord knowed what it was to work.
> He knowed how to pray.
> Ma Lord's life was trouble, too,
> Trouble ever day.

Hughes said that this poem implies "that when religion places itself at the service of mankind, particularly the humble people, it can . . . strengthen them and guide them."

Four of Hughes's poems, by concentrating upon the religious be-

[1] In order to place chronologically Hughes's treatments of different religious themes and his disclosures of personal attitudes, the dates of first publication follow initial references to poems.

liefs of the protagonists, reveal his own point of view only obliquely, if at all. The best of them is "Judgment Day" (1927), which dramatizes the imagination of a simple Black person whose soul has gone "flyin' to de stars an' moon / A shoutin' God, I's comin' soon." And in heaven the protagonist, "clean an' bright," hears his kindly, anthropomorphized Lord say "don't be 'fraid / Cause you ain't dead." A similarly faithful worshipper, shown when "a black old woman croons / In the amen-corner of the / Ebecaneezer Baptist Church," is briefly presented in "Prayer Meeting" (1923). In neither of these poems does Hughes give the slightest indication of his own beliefs. Nor does he do so tangibly through his protagonists in the other two poems of this group, "Sinner" (1927) and "Acceptance" (1957). These two, although separated by thirty years, function almost as companion pieces: the former in five lines confidently asks God for mercy, and the latter in four lines assumes that mercy is always forthcoming; the syntax of the former allows for the infusion of the author's own voice, as does the diction of the latter. An early poem on the fringe of this group, "Prayer" (1925), finds the young author sincerely shading what seems his own voice into that of the speaker:

> I ask you this:
> Which way to go?
> I ask you this:
> Which sin to bear?
> Which crown to put
> Upon my hair?
> I do not know,
> Lord God,
> I do not know.

The largest category within Hughes's poems containing religious references is comprised of pieces that are ambiguous, if one is searching for Hughes's degree of piety; that is, in portraying Black experience, they simply "tell it like it is." Of the ten poems involved, published at various times between 1927 and 1964, I believe three should be noted. One, "Freedom's Plow" (1943), deserves attention for a negative reason: in its seven pages on the founding and development of America, its only concession to the pious is that "prayer-makers" were among those who built the nation. Two other poems are enlivened by humor: "Madam and the Number Writer" (1943) and

"Who But the Lord?" (1947). In the former, Hughes's well-known character Madame Alberta K. Johnson whimsically swears off playing the numbers in Harlem in favor of heaven's "golden streets / Where the number not only / Comes out—but repeats!" Another experience of Harlemites, police brutality, is scored along with the foot-dragging of the Lord after the protagonist's cry for His immediate help:

> But the Lord he was not quick.
> The Law raised up his stick
> And beat the living hell
> Out of me!

A reference to two early poems might serve as a reminder that the works under consideration belong primarily to an artistic rather than a religious tradition. "Caribbean Sunset" (1926), offering a startling example of the kind of "literary conceit" popular in the seventeenth century, dramatizes the sunset as God's hemorrhage. And mixing ancient topographical form with modern Black folk speech and hymnal rhythm, "Angels Wings" (1927) itself exhibits the physical shape of its subject.

Among those poems that leave less doubt about Hughes's religious philosophy, three written in the 1950s sympathetically emphasize mankind in the positivistic alliance of God, man, and nature. In "Café: 3 A.M." (1951), the poet sees "God, Nature, / or somebody" as responsible for the creation of perverts under police surveillance. In "Pastoral" (1958), he is compassionate toward simple people who believe they see the Savior in clouds, heaven's tears in dew, and Jesus' souvenirs in flowers. And in "Litany" (1959), he pleads that divine love be extended to those who expect none:

> The sick, the depraved,
> The desperate, the tired,
> All the scum
> Of our weary city
> Gather up
> In the arms of your pity.

Black people speaking for themselves in addressing God are supported in Hughes's poetry, especially when they do it in song. He finds personal and ancestral, rocklike strength in the music that furnishes the title of "Spirituals" (1944). "Sunday prayers syncopate glory" in "Consider Me" (1951); and the tambourines-to-glory theme struck off in "Tambourines" (1959) is defended in its middle stanza: "A gospel shout / And a gospel song: / Life is short / *But God is long!*"

It is the celebration of that life, short though it might be, that invigorates much of Hughes's poetry. Seven poems, distributed through twenty-five years of his career, give ethical dimension to human vitality. "Saturday Night" (1926), "Fire" (1927), "Sylvester's Dying Bed" (1931), and "Sunday by the Combination" (1951) all concern good-timing sinners and sweet papas who lived robustly until "the Lawd put out the light." Divine sanction is attributed to happiness and friendliness in "Heaven" (1941). On the other hand, "Young Sailor" (1926) and "Democracy" (1943) make personal dynamism and political liberty indispensable to man's only heaven, an earthly one. Two lines from the latter poem clarify this theme of the poet's: "I do not need my freedom when I'm dead. / I cannot live on tomorrow's bread."

Religion has been especially valuable to Black people, Hughes's poetry suggests, in its toughening of that life force just mentioned. Two of his best early poems, "Brass Spittoons" (1926) and "The Negro Mother" (1931), celebrate a racial endurance encouraged by religious faith. In the 1965 interview, Hughes spoke of the former poem as

> growing out of a childhood memory of my own while yet living in Kansas; I believe that I was in the eighth grade and I worked for a time in one of the hotels in Lawrence, and had to, myself, clean the old brass spittoons that they used in those days.

Just as slaves found positive uses for an equivocal Christianity, the young porter in "Brass Spittoons," beleaguered by what seems like mountains of white men's scornful commands, works up this confidence: "A bright bowl of brass is beautiful to the / Lord." In the justifiably popular "The Negro Mother," the slavemasters' ambiguous religion has become more resolution than ritual in the mind of the archetypal speaker:

> I am the one who labored as a slave,
> Beaten and mistreated for the work that I gave—
> Children sold away from me, husband sold, too.
> No safety, no love, no respect was I due.

Three hundred years in the deepest South:
But God put a song and a prayer in my mouth.
God put a dream like steel in my soul.

The other two poems that adopt this theme, "Graduation" (1945) and "Deferred" (1958), are mediocre by comparison. The former begins with an appealing sensory burst, but deserves mention only for its theme: *"Praise Jesus! / The colored race will rise!"*—will rise presumably because the Lord fosters Black ambition.

Comparisons between the fate of Jesus and the revilement of Black people appear both early and late in Hughes's poetry. Two of the late references are found in *Ask Your Mama* (1961): in "Gospel Cha Cha," the protagonist sees himself mirrored in the Crucifixion, and in "Show Fare, Please," the speaker ends the book by connecting his humanity with the Holy Trinity ("Of these three, / Is one / Me?"). The Holy Crucifixion, in fact, is Hughes's most constant reference in linking Black people with Christ. "Ballad of Mary's Son" (1958), by applying the phrase "Mary's Boy" to a young Black man lynched during Passover and by calling Christ "Mary's Son," merges their persons in a shared, spiritual tragedy.

Hughes's unique, never-anthologized "Christ in Alabama" (1931) reveals his strongest response to the racist evils that have long out-faced American Christianity. His first reading of the poem, at the University of North Carolina on November 21, 1931, stimulated threats of violence from whites. The origin of the short poem, in fact, had been recent violence—physical, psychological, and judicial—visited upon Black people. About ten days earlier at Hampton Institute in Virginia, Dorothy Maynor, then a student choir singer, had told the poet of two instances: Hampton's new football coach had just been beaten to death by an Alabama mob for accidentally stationing his car in a "white" parking lot, and Fisk University's Dean of Women, Juliette Derricotte (whom Hughes had known in Paris and New York), had died the same weekend from an auto crash in rural Georgia after being refused aid in a nearby "white" hospital. And the miasma of the infamous Scottsboro Case had personally enveloped Hughes, who had altered his current poetry-reading itinerary in the South to recite some of his work to the nine young victims in jail.

In *I Wonder As I Wander,* Hughes records that his ironic "Christ in Alabama" develops the thought of "how Christ, with no human father, would be accepted were He born in the South of a Negro mother." The poem opens with "Christ is a nigger, / Beaten and black: / Oh, bare your back!" and ends with

> Most Holy Bastard
> Of the bleeding mouth:
> Nigger Christ
> On the cross of the South!

The serious truth represented in this poem is part of American history, just as the shock and outrage occasioned by its delivery in 1931 have remained part of the racial anomalies in the white American psyche. The capitalization in this original version hardly elevates "Bastard" to the level of divinity. The term is purely genetic, as one can see by considering Hughes's long interest in the problems of mixed blood, as well as the original title ("Bastard of Gold") of his rather sentimental story published several years later, "African Morning." And although calling Christ "Nigger" infuriated some of Hughes's original audience, numberless Black and Christian martyrdoms support the usage—just as society's suppression of white student activists and white revolutionaries has caused a few essayists in America and Europe to write of the latter as "niggers."

The *Atlanta World* of December 18, 1931, contains Hughes's explanation of the seeming impiety for which local Carolinians insisted that he be run out of town:

> . . . anything which makes people think of existing evil conditions is worthwhile. Sometimes in order to attract attention somebody must embody these ideas in sensational forms. I meant my poem to be a protest against the domination of all stronger peoples over weaker ones.

The word "protest," incidentally, like the poem's sensational content, might diminish one's perception of its artistic merit. Its economical selectivity of phrasing, accomplished with a genuine flair for acrostics in the first nine of its fourteen lines, is notable.

Even though the poet does not disproportionately blame religious institutions for society's transgressions, he specifies failures of the church. And in doing so, he implies that Black churches have special obligations. In "High to Low" (1949) and "Projection" (1951), for example, he criticizes their exclusivity and other divisive standards.

The protagonist in "High to Low," expressing a middle-class snob-
bery, speaks contemptuously of "the way you shout out loud in
church, / (not St. Phillips)." Using his own voice in "Projection,"
Hughes hopes for "that day when Abyssinia Baptist Church / throws
her enormous arms around / St. James Presbyterian," adding that
"on that day— / Do, Jesus! / Manhattan Island will whirl / like a
Dizzy Gillespie transcription."

Usually, however, Hughes's poetic references to his own opinion
are more cynical than hopeful; and almost half of the barbs launched
in his own voice or attitude, rather than in that of another protagonist, are aimed at Black churchmen. The clerics' overemphasis
upon the collection plate is rather humorously scored in "Sunday
Morning Prophecy" (1942), an expertly cadenced rendering of an
old Black minister's vivid sermonizing. In "Ballad of the Man Who's
Gone" (1942) and "Night Funeral in Harlem" (1951), the preachers'
concentration on their service charges makes them seem less humane
than their Black customers who, the poet concludes, are so poor that
they *"ain't got / No business to die."*

Somewhat comparable—although not qualitatively—to "Christ
in Alabama" is a poem that, in the 1930s and 1940s especially, attracted misinterpretation and malicious resentment: "Goodbye
Christ" (1932). Typically, among other results, the author was barred
from speaking at a Los Angeles YMCA in 1935, was picketed by the
America First Party while speaking at Wayne State University in
1943, and, fifteen years later, was still explaining that the poem was
"an ironic protest against racketeering in the churches" and was
"anti-misuse of religion" (in the *Vancouver Sun*, December 3, 1958).
The central thrust, referring to the New Testament, is in these lines:

> But it's dead now.
> The popes and the preachers've
> Made too much money from it.
> They've sold you [Christ] to too many
> Kings, generals, robbers, and killers—

and the main reference to Black churches specifies "big black Saint
Becton / Of the Consecrated Dime," the Harlem preacher exposed
as a charlatan in Hughes's *The Big Sea*. A Black minister from Detroit (the Reverend Charles C. Hill), to counter the picketing and
circularizing by the forces of Gerald L. K. Smith, gave the *Michigan
Chronicle* of May 8, 1943, an opinion that would not be uncommon

in the 1970s: "I can join Langston Hughes with teeming others in saying 'Goodbye Christ'—the Christ as held up by the white supremacists."

Among Hughes's cynical poems that criticize white supremacists' abuse of religion, "Bible Belt" (1966) ironically echoes "Christ in Alabama" by pointing out that if Jesus were to return to earth as a Black man, He would be refused entrance to many public places. Christianity is useless against racism in both America and Africa, according to "Blues in Stereo" (1961), in ghettoes and huts where "the white God never goes." It is more obviously useless in American-style tragedies denoted by the title of "Bombings in Dixie" (1966), in which Hughes avers that mourning and praying are inadequate responses. It is indeed useless when a man's immediate, practical needs are continually denied, as the poet prosaically declares in "Go Slow" (1966) in the following excerpt:

> Am I supposed to be God,
> Or an angel with wings
> And a halo on my head
> While jobless I starve dead?

Religion might be a solace at times, the poet says in "Luck" (1947), but getting "only heaven" is a scant achievement.

Rarely does the poet use a voice or attitude other than his own to convey cynicism about religion. But in one of his best poems, "Song for a Dark Girl" (1927), he does so:

> Way Down South in Dixie
> (Break the heart of me)
> They hung my black young lover
> To a cross roads tree.
>
> Way Down South in Dixie
> (Bruised body high in air)
> I asked the white Lord Jesus
> What was the use of prayer.
>
> Way Down South in Dixie
> (Break the heart of me)
> Love is a naked shadow
> On a gnarled and naked tree.

Thematically, the end of the middle stanza condenses the final rhetorical question with which Black people are bound to challenge hypocritical religion in America. Qualitatively, "Song for a Dark Girl" exemplifies some of Hughes's strongest poetic virtues: simplicity (only six different words contain more than one syllable), vivid and appropriate imagery, economy, and social significance. Ironic juxtaposition (an antic Dixieland tune contiguous with Black heartbreak in the refrain) and unforced symbolism ("crossroads" separated into two words to suggest Calvary) are also typical Hughesian techniques worthy of notice. In "Madam and the Minister" (1944), artistically in a lower category, the aforementioned Alberta K. Johnson cynically responds to a clergyman visiting her home to inquire about the state of her soul: "None of your / Business, friend." But Hughes, knowing that only special circumstances would force a Harlemite to speak that way to a minister, concludes the poem with her confession: "I felt kinder sorry / I talked that way / . . . / So I ain't in no mood / For sin today." Her special circumstance is that she is a woman alone in Harlem, struggling with problems that have made her believe (as the poem "Madam and Her Might-Have-Been" reveals):

> When you think you got bread
> It's always a stone—
> Nobody loves nobody
> For yourself alone.

The final category to be mentioned, one of the smallest, is perhaps prefigured in the largest category, the generally undistinguished and ambiguous group concerning the author's attitudes. Only two poems convey what seems to be Hughes's ultimate point of view: that one's religion is his personal affair. "Passing Love" (1927) compares love to religious devotion, with a faint trace of cynicism, but lyrically invests both with delicacy and private beauty. The lines "Because you are to me a prayer / I cannot say you everywhere" perfectly disclose the poet's feelings. "Personal" (1933) tightly compresses Hughes's opinion, early and late in his career, regarding the subject:

> In an envelope marked:
> *Personal*
> God addressed me a letter.
> In an envelope marked:
> *Personal*
> I have given my answer.

In drawing conclusions about the author's accomplishments in these poems, one should avoid superimposing upon Hughes's aims the needs of any later generation. According to the 1965 interview, he wanted primarily to reveal "the folk expression" of Black people in their religion. In doing so, he could not violate his own convictions that food and jobs and housing were interwoven with piety in the ghetto—despite the rhythmical and mystical beauty of church rituals—and that misuse of this combination of beauty and human need was the one "sin" that should be condemned. Within these limitations of subject and attitude, then, one must finally ask the following questions: (1) Do these poems adequately achieve the poet's aim? (2) Do they satisfy today's searchers for Black experience in religious poetry? (3) Do they contain a just proportion of works worth treasuring as cultural legacy?

Regarding the first question, Hughes's achievement of his purpose is fairly comprehensive. He shows the folk, inside and outside the church, happy and sad, in states of apparent grace and in conditions of sin, expressing their shades of piety. Such external church affairs as picnics and such internal ones as baptisms are so numerous that Hughes could not be expected to detail them. But he does dramatize through various individuals—not sociological types—a wide range of those firm beliefs and nuances of attitudes that define religious life.

The second question would ideally be answered by each reader for himself. Many Black readers today are disenchanted with Christianity as a slaveholder's religion updated to genocidal proportions. But for those able to concentrate upon the strengths of their ancestors rather than the tyrannies of white people, Hughes's poems about Black folk of simple faith and unbreakable endurance are staple nourishment.

The final question about these sixty-odd works, their value as legacy, brings to the fore an ideal possibility mentioned early in these remarks: the coexistence in a poem of high quality and treasurable Black experience. Three seem to me to qualify: "Song for a Dark Girl" and "The Negro Mother," both available in Hughes's *Selected Poems,* and "Christ in Alabama," a poem which has been reprinted only three times in forty years, but which gives bold distinction to the poet's last collection, *The Panther and the Lash.* Although most of the poems under discussion are not worth close study, and although a number are technically mediocre, "Brass Spittoons," Judgment Day," and "Passing Love" are also meritorious. "The Negro Mother," which has brought tears to the eyes of many a Black audience, compassionately includes among its injunctions:

> All you dark children in the world out there,
> Remember my sweat, my pain, my despair.
> Remember my years, heavy with sorrow—
> And make of those years a torch for tomorrow.
>
> Lift high my banner out of the dust.
> Stand like free men supporting my trust.
> Believe in the right, let none push you back.
> *Remember the whip and the slaver's track.* (Italics mine.)

The entire poem, legendary in tone and simple in language, is well worth absorbing. And if Black readers take to heart the last-quoted line, they will surely memorize the short poems "Song for a Dark Girl" and "Christ in Alabama." Line-by-line knowledge of "Song for a Dark Girl" will help them to memorialize those thousands of Black men, women, and children who died under the fists, chains, ropes, and firebrands of their white countrymen. Memorization of "Christ in Alabama," with its hammer-drill ending, will help them to sustain a moral equilibrium in their entrapment between a past that cries for vengeance and a future that demands more of that very humanity that America has so cruelly tried to debase.

Thematically, then, Hughes writes with most emotional strength and aptness of form when he records cynicism about religion in America, compares Black experience with the fate of Christ, or unites the religious impulse with his race's determination to survive. His competent work extends also to the dramatization of folk piety, to the celebration of life, and to the lyrical expression of his religious respect.

If future criticism reaffirms that ten percent of Hughes's poems on this general theme do indeed permanently merit either attention or admiration, it can be said that he labored well while writing for bread. It is already incontestable that, although his own testimony reveals that he worked usually with ease and often with rapidity, he wrote, even on this sensitive theme, with honesty and with the intent to preserve in literature the dignity, as well as the reality, of ordinary people.

# I Do Not Marvel, Countee Cullen

## by Eugenia W. Collier

Back in the 20's a young colored poet wrote:

> Strange,
> That in this nigger place
> I should meet life face to face;
> When, for years, I had been seeking
> Life in places gentler-speaking,
> Until I came to this vile street
> And found Life stepping on my feet! [1]

The young Langston Hughes was expressing here the verve, the vibrancy of the black mecca which became the gatheringplace of many creative young Negroes during the turbulent decade after World War I. From the farms and towns and metropolitan centers of the South and Mid-West came these young people, most of them seeking the economic opportunities of the big city, many of them seeking to discover the secrets of the city in order to transpose them into artistic expressions more numerous and more lovely than Negro America had produced before.

These were restless times. The 1920's are remembered as America's era of high living and bathtub gin, of fortunes made and eventually lost on the stock market. But for Negro Americans there was little high living. These were years of seeking—years in which Negroes not only felt keenly the injustice of their numerous social and cultural deprivations, but also felt compelled to improve their lot. They had helped to fight the war to make the world safe for

"I Do Not Marvel, Countee Cullen," by Eugenia W. Collier. From *CLA Journal*, XI (September 1967), 73–87. Copyright © 1967 by the College Language Association. Reprinted by permission of the author and the publisher.

[1] Langston Hughes' "Esthete in Harlem" in James Weldon Johnson's *The Book of American Negro Poetry* (New York, 1931), p. 239.

democracy, and were now wondering how to make this democracy
safe for dark Americans. Consequently, many Negroes migrated
northward to the cities, seeking education, jobs and relative freedom
from social restrictions. With increasing vehemence, Negroes pressed
for civil rights, which were too slow in coming. Meanwhile race riots
darkened the summers of the decade. Leaders like W. E. Burghardt
DuBois, James Weldon Johnson and William Stanley Braithwaite
were encouraging a new articulation and a new self-respect. The
Negro was emerging from his dark cocoon. And in what better place
could this emergence occur than in Harlem?—home of 175,000 Negroes—Negroes of many different backgrounds and abilities, but all
sharing the onus—and the artistic advantage—of color.

The first flowering occurred in poetry. In 1919, after the Chicago
race riot in which 38 people were killed, over 500 were injured, and
over 1000 families were left homeless,[2] an intense young man from
Jamaica, one Claude McKay, published this account in a New York
newspaper:

> If we must die—let it not be like hogs
> Hunted and penned in an inglorious spot,
> While round us bark the mad and hungry dogs,
> Making their mock at our accursed lot,
> If we must die—oh, let us nobly die,
> So that our precious blood may not be shed
> In vain; then even the monsters we defy
> Shall be constrained to honor us though dead!
> Oh kinsmen! We must meet the common foe;
> Though far outnumbered, let us show us brave,
> And for their thousand blows deal one death blow!
> What though before us lies the open grave?
> Like men we'll face the murderous cowardly pack,
> Pressed to the wall, dying but fighting back! [3]

Strong, masculine poetry this, setting the tone for the poetry of
the New Negro. How different this was from the dialect poetry of
the Dunbar school, and from the decorous, ivy-tower poetry of the
colored scholar-poets! Here was a strong expression of self-respect,
of a sense of one's own identity in spite of ego-shattering forces.
Moreover, the poem transcends the instance of this particular Ne-

[2] W. Cooper, "Claude McKay and the New Negro Poets of the 20's," *Phylon*
(Fall, 1964), p. 300.
[3] Johnson, *op. cit.*, p. 168.

gro in battle with these particular white tormenters. It sounds a universal note; it is the voice of indomitable courage in the face of chaos. Years later, when England faced the hell of German bombings, Winston Churchill bolstered his people's courage by quoting this very poem.

"If We Must Die," then, demonstrates some of the principal characteristics of the poetry which later issued from Harlem and soon radiated to certain young poets writing in other parts of the nation. Negro poets were turning inward and outward simultaneously. They looked within themselves, to Negro culture and experience, for subject matter. They used diverse techniques: some used traditional poetic forms, some used forms adapted from the blues and spirituals, some created unique forms. And the best poetry of the period groped toward an expression of universal truth, which applied not only to that time and that place and these Negroes, but also to people everywhere from the dawn of civilization.

Literary historians and critics have a way of saying that the Negro poet faces a dilemma: Should he write as a Negro, or should he write as an American? They seem to mean, should he write poetry of social protest, or is he free to write of love and nature and God? I am convinced that this dilemma is only a straw man, created by the critics themselves.

Of course, Negro poets write of other subjects than social protest. Of the poets of the Harlem Renaissance, the fiery McKay wrote gentle lyrics of love, and tender poems of his childhood in Jamaica. Countee Cullen's delicate sonnets of love and life are among the most beautiful produced by the America of his time. Anne Spencer, writing in Lynchburg, produced lovely, feminine poetry on a wide range of subjects.

But for the Negro poet, from the slave poet Jupiter Hammon to our contemporary Julian Bond and LeRoi Jones, race is a basic and primary truth. In an article in *Phylon* in 1950, Gwendolyn Brooks said: "Every Negro poet has 'something to say.' Simply because he is a Negro, he cannot escape having important things to say. His mere body, for that matter, is an eloquence. His quiet walk down the street is a speech to the people. Is a rebuke, is a plea, is a school." [4]

---

[4] Quoted in Gwendolyn Brooks' Foreword to Langston Hughes' *New Negro Poets: USA* (Bloomington, Indiana, 1964), p. 13.

I submit that in those instances when the Negro poet effectively uses the advantages of his racial experience, combined with a high degree of artistry, he is writing the most American poetry possible. In his protest against hatred and injustice, in his pride in himself, in his quest for social and economic equality, he is expressing both the feelings and the logic which the Founding Fathers expressed in the Declaration of Independence; he is expressing the hope of the immigrant seeing the Statue of Liberty for the first time; he is, in short, voicing the American Dream. The Harlem Renaissance saw the first abundant outpouring of such poetry.

Since it is not possible for us here today to examine all, or even most of this poetry, I thought we might look in depth at three poems that represent some of the principal themes of the Negro poetry of the 1920's, and to cite incidentally other poems which deal effectively with these themes.

It seems to me that a poem which effectively expresses the spirit of Harlem Renaissance poetry is "From the Dark Tower," by Countee Cullen. It is a restrained, dignified, poignant work, influenced in form by Keats and Shelley rather than by the moderns. Incidentally, The Dark Tower was actually a place on 136th Street in Harlem, where a number of the poets used to gather. Perhaps Cullen knew he was speaking for the others, too, when he wrote:

> We shall not always plant while others reap
> The golden increment of bursting fruit,
> Not always countenance, abject and mute
> That lesser men should hold their brothers cheap;
> Not everlastingly while others sleep
> Shall we beguile their limbs with mellow flute,
> Not always bend to some more subtle brute;
> We were not made eternally to weep.
>
> The night whose sable breast relieves the stark
> White stars is no less lovely being dark,
> And there are buds that cannot bloom at all
> In light, but crumple, piteous, and fall;
> So in the dark we hide the heart that bleeds,
> And wait, and tend our agonizing seeds.[5]

Let us examine the symbolism contained in the poem. Here we have the often-used symbol of planting seeds and reaping fruit. This

---

[5] Johnson, *op. cit.*, p. 228.

symbol invariably refers to the natural sequence of things—the hope
eventually realized, or the "just deserts" finally obtained. The sow-
ing-reaping symbol here effectively expresses the frustration that
inevitably falls to the individual or group of people caught in an
unjust system. The image of a person planting the seeds of his
labor, knowing even as he plants that "others" will pluck the fruit,
is a picture of the frustration which is so often the Negro's lot. The
image necessarily (and perhaps unconsciously) implies certain questions: What must be the feelings of the one who plants? How long
will he continue to plant without reward? Will he not eventually
stop planting, or perhaps begin seizing the fruit which is rightfully
his? In what light does he see himself? How does he regard the
"others" who "reap the golden increment of bursting fruit"? What
physical and emotional damage results to the laborer from this ar-
rangement to which obviously he never consented?

In his basic symbol, then, Cullen expresses the crux of the protest
poem which so flourished in the Harlem Renaissance. In poem after
poem, articulate young Negroes answered these questions or asked
them again, these questions and many more. And in the asking, and
in the answering, they were speaking of the old, well-worn (though
never quite realized) American ideals.

In the octave of the poem, Cullen answers some of these questions.
The grim promise "not always" tolls ominously like an iron bell
through the first eight lines. "We shall not always plant while others
reap," he promises. By degrees he probes deeper and deeper into
the actual meaning of the image. In the next two lines he points
out one of many strange paradoxes of social injustice: that the
"abject and mute" victim must permit himself to be considered
inferior by "lesser men"—that is, men who have lost a measure of
their humanity because they have degraded their brothers. This
image is a statement of a loss of human values—the "abject and
mute" victim of an unjust social system, bereft of spirit, silently
serving another who has himself suffered a different kind of loss in
robbing his fellow man of his potential—that is, the fruit of his
seed. Perhaps this destruction of the human spirit is the "more
subtle brute" of which the poet speaks. The last line of the octave
promises eventual change in the words, "We were not made eter-
nally to weep." Yet it implies that relief is still a long way off.

It is in the sestet that the poem itself blossoms into full-blown dark beauty. With the skill of an impressionist painter, the poet juxtaposes black and white into a canvas of brilliant contrasts. The night is pictured as being beautiful because it is dark—a welcome relief from the stark whiteness of the stars. The image suggests the pride in Negritude which became important in the Harlem Renaissance—the pride in the physical beauty of black people, the Negro folk culture which has enriched America, the strength which the Negro has earned through suffering. Cullen describes the night as being not only a lovely thing, but also a sheltering thing. The image of the buds that cannot bloom in light suggests that the Negro's experience has created a unique place for him in American culture: there are songs that he alone can sing.

The final couplet combines the beautiful and sheltering concept of darkness with the basic symbol of futile planting. The poet now splashes a shocking red onto his black and white canvas. The dark becomes not only a shelter for developing buds, but also a place to conceal gaping wounds. These two lines are quiet but extremely disturbing: "So in the dark we hide the heart that bleeds, / And wait, and tend our agonizing seeds." And the reader cannot help wondering, what sort of fruit will grow from these "agonizing seeds"?

Cullen's sonnet is one of the best produced by the Harlem Renaissance. Not every poet had Cullen's technical control over his medium, even over the exacting sonnet form. Yet with varying degrees of skill and with differing emphasis on various aspects, variations appeared on the themes that issued from the Dark Tower. Arna Bontemps used the agrarian symbol in "A Black Man Talks of Reaping." Fenton Johnson years before had captured the utter despair of thwarted potential in "Tired." Claude McKay points out the quiet desperation of ceaseless and hopeless toil in "The Tired Worker." Langston Hughes treats with gentle humor the dignity and importance of the humble worker in "Brass Spittoons." Sterling Brown in "Old Lem" adapts a folk poem into a work of art to protest the system in which the toil of the worker is exploited.

Cullen's concept of black as being beautiful was not unique. Along with his increasing conviction of *who* he was and *what* he was, the Negro poet gained a realization that in the experience of the black masses was rich material for poetic expression. More and more, then, he turned to the music, the ballads, and the folklore that were his heritage. As he used the subject matter of the folk as a vehicle for his poetry, the Negro poet also began to utilize the language of the people.

In order to appreciate the difference between the folk idiom and the traditional dialect, one needs to delve a bit into literary history. After the Civil War, white local colorists turned out work after work concerning antebellum days on the old plantation. Most of these works mourned the past glory of the South and the slave system. With such stars in his eyes, naturally the white apologist could not see and therefore could not portray the Negro as he was. The folk Negro, then, was a cute-talking darky happy with ole massa and the cotton, frolicking through endless Christmas parties. He spoke in a dialect constituted mainly of misspellings, and that revealed him as a pathetic or a humorous character, but certainly not as a genuine human being. Paul Laurence Dunbar and other Negro poets of his time imitated these white authors, instead of using their inside track on Negro experience, so that although their poems were sympathetic to the Negro, they too smacked of the stereotype and were unable to give a true or artistic picture of the actual Negro.

The poets of the Dunbar school, then, found themselves in the peculiar situation of imitating white authors' imitation of Negroes. The New Negro poets of the 20's threw off his yoke of artificiality and looked to the people both for subject matter and for the language in which to express it. The poetry of the Harlem Renaissance is enriched by the strains of the blues, the sweet minor-key melodies of the spirituals, the vigor of the ballads.

One of the most enthusiastic appreciators of folk culture was Sterling A. Brown, a young professor of English. He seems to have absorbed the spirit of the folk as well as their language and experience. One of his most successful folk poems is "The Odyssey of Big Boy," in which the poet has created an art ballad, uniting several aspects of folk experience. The form is the simple, melodious form of the genuine folk ballad, with its sparkling rhythm, its brevity of line, its regular repetition of the fourth line. The language is not the stilted misspelling of Dunbar dialect, but rather is the vibrant, racy speech of actual people. The Negro idiom flows naturally and effectively.

Such form and such language are harmonious with the content. The title announces that this is an odyssey, thereby suggesting a hero of classic proportions, wandering through a mythic world. But the hero has no such classic designation as Ulysses or Odysseus; the hero is called "Big Boy," and somehow you know from the title that Big Boy has *got* to be colored.

Big Boy begins by referring to legendary Negro heroes, expressing his admiration for "such like men"—that is, men of action, men who did things and to whom things happened. Then Big Boy sings of his own travels through America. And, indeed, they have constituted an odyssey. As Big Boy extolls the various jobs he has done in many states, he becomes a symbol of the labor which builds nations. He sings unsentimentally of lifelong toil and hardship in a way typical of folk ballads when he says:

> Done skinned as a boy in Kentucky hills
> Druv steel dere as a man,
> Done stripped tobacco in Virginia's fiel's
>    Alongst de River Dan,
>       Alongst de River Dan;
>
> Done mined de coal in West Virginia
> Liked dat job jes' fine
> Till a load o' slate curved roun' my head
>    Won't work in no mo' mine;
>       Won't work in no mo' mine;

Like the typical folk hero, Big Boy has had numerous successful adventures in sex. He brags lustily of the quantity and quality of his partners, without sentiment, but with humor:

> Had stovepipe blonde in Macon,
>    Yaller gal in Marylan'
> In Richmond had a chocklit brown
>    Called me huh monkey man—
>    Huh big fool monkey man.
>
> Had two fair browns in Arkansaw
> And three in Tennessee
> Had Creole gal in New Orleans
>    Sho Gawd did two time me—
>    Lawd two time, fo' time me—[6]

Big Boy has no great regrets, offers no deep philosophy. Having seen and done a number of things, he asks only to be counted among "such like men" as Casey Jones and Stagolee.

[6] *Ibid.*, p. 247.

The poet thus had used as his raw materials the ballad form, the language and subject matter of the folk. He has suffused them with the spirit of Whitman and polished them into a work of art. Sterling Brown uses folk material in some of his best poems. "Long Gone," like "Odyssey of Big Boy," uses the ballad as a basis for portraying the colored laborer—and loverman. "Frankie and Johnny" parodies the well-known folk ballad to express strong social protest of the sexual taboos of the South. In "Tin Roof Blues" the poet uses the blues form to describe the loneliness of the rural Negro who has migrated to the city. A most effective poem, "Strong Men," intersperses the words of the spirituals with straight-English words to picture the past degradation, the present sufferings, and future promise of the American Negro.

Other poets, too, effectively use folk material. James Weldon Johnson captures the energy and idiom of the old-time Negro preacher in seven verse sermons, *God's Trombones*. Langston Hughes adapts the blues in numerous works. Folk culture, then, proved a fruitful source for artistic expression in Harlem Renaissance poetry.

Perhaps the poems which showed most effectively the tragic consequences of oppression, and which speak most eloquently in a universal language, are the poems which present quick portraits of black individuals. Here one sees a close-up of the laborer in Cullen's poem, who must toil incessantly only to have his golden fruit snatched by others. With great frequency the New Negro poets focused on the individual—often a black woman—and suggest the immense human potential behind the toil of the washer-woman, the strutting and wiggling of the prostitute, the swagger of the dandy, and so forth—human potential that has been destroyed by the social system. Among the best of these is McKay's "The Harlem Dancer."

> Applauding youths laughed with young prostitutes
> And watched her perfect, half-clothed body sway;
> Her voice was like the sound of blended flutes
> Blown by black players upon a picnic day.
> She sang and danced on gracefully and calm,
> The light gauze hanging loose about her form;
> To me she seemed a proudly swaying palm
> Grown lovelier for passing through a storm.

Upon her swarthy neck black, shiny curls
Profusely fell and, tossing coins in praise;
The wine-fused, bold-eyed boys and even the girls,
Devoured her with their eager, passionate gaze;
But looking at her falsely-smiling face,
I knew her self was not in that strange place.[7]

In the slow, measured dignity of the sonnet form McKay has
encased the wild and lascivious world of the Harlem nightclub. As
we study the poem in some depth, we see that this apparent paradox
is actually quite appropriate.

Our first impression of the dancer is gained through a glimpse
of her audience—young people, already caught up in the sordid
life of the city. The men who applaud are mere youths; the prosti-
tutes with them are also young. They applaud and laugh and watch
the suggestive motions of the beautiful, half-revealed body. Yet the
slow-moving rhythm of the poem implies a kind of sadness that
contrasts with their gaiety. Focusing now upon the dancer herself,
the poet compares her voice with the sound of a musical instrument—not with the wail of a saxophone, nor the blatancy of brass,
but with the softly delicate music of "blended flutes." In the next
line the nightclub begins to fade out as the poet places the flutes
on the lips of "black players on a picnic day." The outdoor whole-
someness of a picnic contrasts with the nightclub. The next two
lines imbue the dancer with classic beauty and simplicity; her grace,
her quiet loveliness, her garments draped loosely about her, could
easily belong to Greek sculpture. But the poet compares her instead
to a graceful palm tree, proudly swaying. In this comparison McKay
suggests the pride in their African heritage which was widely expressed by the Harlem poets. The rest of the comparison, describing the palm as "lovelier for passing through a storm," suggests
that the hardships of the dancer's experience have endowed her with
a kind of beauty that she might not otherwise have attained.

Then abruptly the poet brings us back to the reality of the
Harlem nightclub. The coins "tossed in praise" indicate that the
world—and she herself—tragically underestimate her worth. She
dances for mere coins, casually tossed by liquor-befogged youngsters.
The poet reminds us that they, too, are victims, for although they

[7] *Ibid.,* p. 169.

are "wine-fused" and "bold-eyed," they are still only boys and girls. Perhaps their hunger and their eager passion may not be for sex alone, but actually for fulfillment of another sort. In the final couplet, the poet expresses the theme of the poem: that human values can be obscured by economic and social deprivation, but that they persist and are discernible to the compassionate observer.

Now the appropriateness of the sonnet form becomes apparent. Iambic pentameter is a slow, dignified meter, contemplative and often sad; and the theme of the poem is not lascivious dancing, but human dignity, not midnight gaiety but unobtrusive tragedy. The rhyme scheme of the sonnet is demanding and restrictive; so also are the social and economic forces that have shaped the life of the Harlem dancer. There is, then, no conflict between form and theme.

In spite of occasional awkward juxtapositions of words, the poem attains a high level of artistry. The language is dynamic but restrained, the imagery is effective, the emotion is sincere and well-expressed. And although the characters and settings are Negro, the poem has universal application. In vividness it matches the quick, sympathetic portraits of Edwin Arlington Robinson. In social commentary it approaches Edwin Markham's "The Man With the Hoe."

Actually several typical themes radiate from this poem. The interest in Africa is the subject of many poems such as two poems, both called "Heritage," by Countee Cullen and Helene Johnson. And the sordid side of city life is frequently the subject matter of New Negro poetry, much to the chagrin of squeamish middle-class Negro critics.

The black archetype was frequently sketched by the New Negro poets. As a matter of fact, the format became almost overused: that is, the poet looks at a Negro in some negative circumstance; this Negro reminds the poet of Africa (usually a romanticized Africa), and the splendors of the black man in his natural habitat contrasts sharply with the Negro created by America.

In the hands of a skilled poet, this contrast could be made most effective. For example, Waring Cuney expresses economically and well the splendid human potentialities which are hidden beneath the drabness of everyday toil in his poem "No Images."

> She does not know
> Her beauty,

> She thinks her brown body
> Has no glory
>
> If she could dance
> Naked,
> Under palm trees
> And see her image in the river
> She would know.
>
> But there are no palm trees
> On the street,
> And dish water gives back no images.[8]

With varying degrees of skill and universality the Negro poets contributed to American literature a panorama of brown-skinned characters, reminding us of the hidden beauty of ordinary people. We see this in such characters as Gwendolyn Bennett's "Dark Girl," the washer-women of Otto Leland Bohanan and Langston Hughes, the Black Magdalene of Countee Cullen, the patent-leather-haired dandy of Helene Johnson, the dead Effie of Sterling Brown and Langston Hughes' unforgettable Midnight Nan whom the poet admonishes, "Strut and wiggle, Midnight Nan / Wouldn't no good guy be your man." Perhaps the warmest and happiest portrait can be found in a poem by Helene Johnson, the youngest of the New Negro poets of the Renaissance period:

> Little brown boy,
> Slim, dark, big eyed,
> Crooning love songs to your banjo
> Down at the Lafayette—
> Gee, boy, I love the way you hold your head,
> High sort of and a bit to one side,
> Like a prince, a jazz prince, and I love
> Your eyes flashing, and your hands,
> And your patent-leathered feet
> And your shoulders jerking the jig-wa
> And I love your teeth flashing,
> And the way your hair shines in the spotlight
> Like it was the real stuff.
> Gee, brown boy, I loves you all over.

[8] *Ibid.*, p. 283.

I'm glad I'm a jig. I'm glad I can
Understand your dancin' and your
Singin', and feel all the happiness
And joy and don't care in you.
Gee, boy, when you sing, I can close my ears
And hear tomtoms just as plain.
Listen to me, will you, what do I know
About tomtoms? But I like the word, sort of,
Don't you? It belongs to us.
Gee, boy, I love the way you hold your head,
And the way you sing and dance,
And everything.
Say, I think you're wonderful. You're
All right with me,
You are.[9]

Like the other poetic portraits, this happy little poem, written in the idiom of the street, expresses a fierce pride in things Negro, finds dignity, beauty and worth in the commonplace. Almost all of the poetic portraits contain a measure of social protest. Sometimes the protest is direct and militant; sometimes it is restrained; often it is merely implied. Almost always, it is there.

I think, in fact, that in seeking to determine the significance of the best poetry of the Harlem Renaissance as a whole, we might emphasize this very point: The New Negro poets discovered and expressed a deep pride in being black. This expression took shape in several ways: First, in their extolling of Africa, the place of their origin; second, in their use of black culture—that is, spirituals, blues, and ballads—for content and form; third, in their change from the false dialect of the Dunbar school to the idiom of the people; fourth, in their attempt to portray realistically the world of the black American. Although these poets wrote many fine poems that did not concern racial themes, their most significant works were the ones that used Negro experience as a vehicle for their art. They produced many good poems, and some excellent ones.

Now, what, actually, is the significance of the Harlem poets? I think that in at least three ways they were extremely significant.

[9] *Ibid.,* pp. 279–280.

In the first place, their works are invaluable to the student of American civilization. Poetry is the artistic revelation of the soul. We cannot listen to a man's prayers, but we can read his poetry. It reveals intimacies of the human condition which prose can never reveal. It tells more about humankind than a psychological study. Poetry by Negroes about Negro experience illuminates a kind of truth about America which simply cannot be told elsewhere. No white author can possibly write it. The person interested in finding out the ingredients of American civilization would do well to study the Harlem poets.

In the second place, these poets contributed a representative body of poems for the inspiration of future Negro poets. They provided a tradition of artistry and truth and pride in being black.

Third, and perhaps most important, these poets sang the American dream. There is no conflict between Negro poetry and American poetry. For these darker children cry out the very essence of American ideals. They insist that "All men are created equal" and are "endowed by their creator with certain inalienable rights." They insist on "brotherhood from sea to shining sea." While the white society denies them the freedom upon which the American dream is based, the dark poets affirm faith in the existence and the rightness of this freedom by demanding their share. And at times this faith in national ideals transcends the nation itself and speaks not of America but of humanity.

I want to close my discussion with a comment upon a famous sonnet by Countee Cullen:

> I doubt not God is good, well-meaning, kind
> And did He stoop to quibble could tell why
> The little buried mole continues blind,
> Why flesh that mirrors Him must some day die,
> Make plain the reason tortured Tantalus
> Is baited by the fickle fruit, declare
> If merely brute caprice dooms Sisyphus
> To struggle up a never-ending stair.
> Inscrutable His ways are, and immune
> To catechism by a mind too strewn
> With petty cares to slightly understand
> What awful brain compels His awful hand.

> Yet do I marvel at this curious thing:
> To make a poet black, and bid him sing! [10]

A lovely poem, by any standards! But my comment is this: *I do not marvel, Countee Cullen,* that God should bid the black poet sing. For who else could sing so well, and who else has such a song?

[10] *Ibid.,* p. 231.

# A Poet's Odyssey: Melvin B. Tolson

TOLSON: This is M. B. Tolson speaking "From My Books." I relive again the last two lines of Keats's famous sonnet, "On Looking into Chapman's Homer," when I recall the exciting Christmas Eve of 1943. It brought me the good news that my first volume of poetry was to be published. I was forty-three years old. I had lived on hope, and, as Robert Lowell says, "Hope lives in doubt." I had kept the faith; but, sometimes, as Lowell says again, "Faith is trying to do without faith."

INTERVIEWER: [1] Since every man is a philosopher, what was your philosophy during those years?

TOLSON: I think my philosophy, at that time on the darkling plain, was summed up in a poem that appeared in my first book, *Rendezvous with America*. The poem was quoted in the *Saturday Review of Literature* when Stephen Vincent Benét reviewed the book. The lyric was called "The Poet." It brings back to me those salad days, like Cleopatra's memories of Caesar after she had fallen in love with Mark Antony.

INTERVIEWER: Do you mind reading the poem?

### THE POET

The poet cheats us with humility.
Ignored by *Who's Who* among his peers
And *Job's News* also, yet this lapidary
Endures the wormwood of anonymous years:
He shapes and polishes chaos without a fee,
The bones of silence fat no pedigree.

His ego is not vain,
Stuffs not on caviar of smile and phrase.
He comes of nobler strain,

[1] The interviewer was M. W. King, professor of English, Lincoln University, Jefferson City, Mo.; the interview took place at Langston University, Langston, Oklahoma, March 10, 1965.

Is marrowed with racier ways:
The beggar Vanity feeds on the crumbs of praise.

He stands before the bar of pride,
Gives not a tinker's dam
For those who flatter or deride
His epic or epigram:
The potboy, not the connoisseur, toadies for a dram.

Peep through his judas-hole
And see the dogma of self at work,
The nerve and verve of soul
That in the sky-born lurk:
The eagle's heart abides not in the mole,
The poppy thrives not at the arctic pole.

A freebooter of lands and seas,
He plunders the dialects of the marketplace,
Thieves lexicons of Crown jewel discoveries,
Pillages the symbols and meccas of the race:
Of thefts the poet's magic leaves no trace.

An Ishmaelite,
He breaks the icons of the Old and New,
Devours your privacy like a parasite,
Parades the skeletons closeted with God and You:
The poet's lien exempts the Many nor the Few.

An anchoret,
He feeds on the raven's bread,
Candles worlds whose suns have set,
Leads Nature to the nuptial bed,
Bathes in pools that never mortals wet:
The poet unlocks the wilderness with an epithet.

A Champion of the People versus Kings—
His only martyrdom is poetry:
A hater of the hierarchy of things—
Freedom's need is his necessity.
The poet flings upon the winds blueprints of Springs:
A bright new world where he alone
    will know work's menacings!

INTERVIEWER: That was over twenty years ago. Would you make any changes now, either in content or in form?

TOLSON: "The only thing that does *not* change is the law that everything changes." The poet-protagonist in the lyric just quoted, Heraclitus, says the poet, any poet in the Greek sense, "shapes and polishes chaos without a fee." He is *poiētēs*—the maker. The word *art* comes from *ars* (to put together)—that is, human contrivance acquired through experience, study, observation, and knack. You know what Ezra Pound did to the original manuscript of T. S. Eliot's *The Waste Land,* bringing order out of chaos. The premise becomes more obvious when we examine the deletions and alterations in Poe's "To Helen" and the first four lines of Yeats's "Leda and the Swan."

INTERVIEWER: One cannot re-do a work of art.

TOLSON: Remember that Cocteau, who said that, *did* re-do his syntax and orthography. Of course, he believed in *Ex*piration instead of *In*spiration— a breathing out of the inner thing. I have tried both of those and also another, in the last fifty years—*Per*spiration. The work sheets of a poet may be very shocking to his starry-eyed admirers. Eliot has expressed for time and eternity the wrestling of Jacob the Poet with his Angel of Words —words that "slip, slide, perish, decay with imprecision, will not stay in place, will not stay still."

INTERVIEWER: Let us come back to this poem, "The Poet," written some twenty years ago. I am not the first to observe in it the striking metaphors that appear in your subsequent books, namely, *The Libretto for the Republic of Liberia* and *Harlem Gallery*. It seems to me that, like the Metaphysical Poets and the French Symbolists, you take an extraordinary delight in figures of speech—especially the metaphor.

TOLSON: I would add another group to the Metaphysicals and the Symbolists: the Negro people. Remember Karl Shapiro's words in his Introduction to *Harlem Gallery*: "Tolson writes in Negro." I am no soothsayer talking to Virgil's dark Aeneas, before his descent into the lower world of the black ghetto; however, I hazard that Shapiro has pillaged my three books and discovered that I, as a black poet, have absorbed the Great Ideas of the Great White World, and interpreted them in the melting-pot idiom of my people. My roots are in Africa, Europe, and America.

INTERVIEWER: I understand that you have lived a varied and, in many instances, a hazardous life?

TOLSON: Tennyson's protagonist says in *Ulysses,* "Much have I seen and known . . ." And, again, "I am a part of all that I have met . . ."—as shoeshine boy, stevedore, soldier, janitor, packinghouse worker, cook on a railroad, waiter in beach-front hotels, boxer, actor, football coach, director of drama, lecturer for the NAACP, organizer of sharecroppers' unions, teacher, father of Ph.D.'s, poet laureate of a foreign country, painter, newspaper columnist, four-time mayor of a town, facer of mobs. I have made my way in the world since I was twelve years old.

INTERVIEWER: Am I to understand that your ideas and images, the blood and bone and sinews of your idiom, have come out of the lives you have led?

TOLSON: Yes. I like to go about places, hobnob with people, gather rich epithets and proverbs in churches and taverns, in cotton fields and dance halls, in streets and toilets. The rhythms and imagery exorcise white magic. The man in the ears is my jack-in-the-box. My catholicity of taste and interest takes in the Charleston and the ballet, Mr. Jelly Roll and Stravinsky, the Congolese sculptor and Phidias, the scop and the Classicist.

INTERVIEWER: I remember the *Partisan Review* observation that, although critics had identified your technique of juxtaposition with Eliot's *Waste Land* and Pound's *Cantos*, its kinship to the associative organization of the blues is obvious.

TOLSON: That acute observation surprised me, for, in the *Libretto*, to which it referred, there was no surface sign of the blues; however, I do write jazz ballads, but the *Libretto* is very literary, to say the least. I thought the Establishment, the Academy, would like it.

INTERVIEWER: Allen Tate said: "For the first time, it seems to me, a Negro poet has assimilated completely the full poetic language of his time and, by implication, the language of the Anglo-American poetic tradition." You "out-pounded Pound," according to Karl Shapiro.

TOLSON: Well, I did go to the Africans instead of the Chinese. Let me read some of those metaphysical African proverbs, in the Fifth Section of the *Libretto*. Gertrude Stein's judgment that the Negro suffers from Nothingness revealed her profound ignorance of African cultures.

*"Seule de tous les continents,"* the parrots
chatter, *"l'Afrique n'a pas d'histoire!"*
*Mon petit doigt me l'a dit:*

"Africa is a rubber ball;
the harder you dash it to the ground,
the higher it will rise.

"A lie betrays its mother tongue.
The Eye said, 'Ear, the Belly is
the foremost of the gods.'

"Fear makes a gnarl a cobra's head.
One finger cannot kill a louse.
The seed waits for the lily.

"No fence's legs are long enough.
The lackey licks the guinea's boot
till holes wear in the tongue.

"A camel on its knees solicits
the ass's load. Potbellies cook
no meals for empty maws.

"When skins are dry the flies go home.
Repentance is a peacock's tail.
The cock is yolk and feed.

"Three steps put man one step ahead.
The rich man's weights are not the poor
man's scales. To each his coole.

"A stinkbug should not peddle perfume.
The tide that ebbs will flow again.
The louse that bites is in

"the inner shirt. An open door
sees both inside and out. The saw
that severs the topmost limb

"comes from the ground. God saves the black
man's soul but not his buttocks from
the white man's lash. The mouse

"as artist paints a mouse that chases
a cat. The diplomat's lie is fat
at home and lean abroad.

"It is the grass that suffers when
two elephants fight. The white man solves
between white sheets his black

"problem. Where would the rich cream be
without skim milk? The eye can cross
the river in a flood.

"Law is a rotten tree; black man, rest
thy weight elsewhere, or like the goat
outrun the white man's stink!"

INTERVIEWER: I can see the reason for the remark by Melville Herskovits [then director of the Program of African Studies at Northwestern University]: "More and more, African modes of creative expression are receiving attention as we seek to understand the thinking of Africans."

TOLSON: Saul Bellow, who was a student under Herskovits, sent his hero, Henderson the Rain King, to Africa to find a cure for the sickness of his soul. "What's past is prologue." Last year Jacob Drachler, teacher and artist, published a book called *African Heritage*. As you probably know,

Mr. Drachler was kind enough to use three sections of my *Libretto* as Prologue, Interlude and Epilogue of this odyssey in African culture.

INTERVIEWER: The Negro has been the victim of ethnic stereotypes. Since you are a realist, may we assume that you take your characters from life?

TOLSON: If the house in which I was born had been located on the other side of town, I would not write about the characters I write about. Selah! In the *Harlem Gallery* I have a few characters from my life, who are designated by name: Louis Armstrong, for example, about whom Hideho Heights, a fictitious character, has composed a poem; however, I cannot vouch for the truth of Hideho's interpretation of Satchmo. The analysis of a real person's tridimensionality is never complete—his biology, his sociology, his psychology. A person may be, from day to day, from mood to mood, from situation to situation, a different jack-in-the-box. So one never knows what figure will be revealed when the lid is removed. This apocalypse of a personality on its Isle of Patmos often shakes the beholder with disbelief. In consternation one may say, sometimes even in terror, "After all these years, I thought I knew him!" To change the metaphor, a person in his lifetime may wear not one mask, but many, which are revelations of his complex nature and nurture. There is no such thing as a flat character in life—stereotypes notwithstanding. The candid camera of intimacy always reveals a personality in the round. People are the fruits —bitter or sweet—of the Heraclitean law of change. A work of art is an illusion of life—a world of make-believe. Its person, place or thing never existed except in the alchemy of the imagination. Yet, I dare say, we understand the people of that other world better than we understand the people of this world. My knowledge of Aeneas, Bloom, Prufrock, Captain Ahab, Othello, and Herzog is more comprehensive than my knowledge of my immediate friends and enemies. Each of these real persons is a multiple jack-in-the-box. Clyde Griffiths in *An American Tragedy* has a clearer identity than Lee Oswald, in spite of the voluminous *Report* of the Warren Commission. In fact, I think Robert Penn Warren could have done a better job in motivation than did Justice Earl Warren. The only Julius Caesar I know is the one Shakespeare created, although I read Julius Caesar's *Commentaries on the Gallic Wars* in the original Latin when I was a fledgling student.

INTERVIEWER: Do you mean that the only persons we can know totally are the characters in fiction—never people in everyday life?

TOLSON: Yes. The abysses of the unconscious are beyond the soundings of even a Freud. Yet, delineations of characters in the poem, the novel, the drama can give us a better understanding of people in a society. In order to get a comprehension of persons and classes, my old professor of sociology used to make his students read and analyze contemporary novels.

It was only then that the cold theories and dead statistics came alive. Before that, they were like the valley of dry bones in the family Bible. By the way, Victor Hugo called the Book of Job the world's greatest tragedy. The aristocratic conception of tragedy comes alive under the black and white magic of Marcel Proust's *Remembrance of Things Past.*

INTERVIEWER: It seems to me, however, that in the seven books that make up this masterpiece, Proust is in large part autobiographical and used models from his fashionable circle as characters.

TOLSON: But a flesh-and-blood model is still a model—not a character in a work of art. An artist is not a photographer, a case-historian. A da Vinci spends several years in the painting of Mona Lisa, constantly trying to capture "the fleeting manifestation of the secret soul of his attractive and winsome subject." A Hollywood cameraman would have done his job in seconds! That great Negro artist Aaron Douglass did a sketch of me. I wanted to use it on the cover of a book, *Harlem Gallery,* but Mrs. Tolson threw up her hands in horror! In a calmer moment, she said it did not look like me. Not at all! That was the very reason I liked it. It did not look like the Tolson that all his friends know when he is wearing one of his masks in society.

INTERVIEWER: I have seen the Douglass sketch, and I agree.

TOLSON: In the *Harlem Gallery* there is a certain Dr. Nkomo: he is an aged African and Africanist who works with The Curator. One day he commented on the difference between a character in life and a character in art.

His *idée fixe* ebbed and flowed across the dinner table:
"Absurd life shakes its ass's ears
in Cendrars'—not Nkomo's—stable.
If,
anchored like hooks of a hag-fish to sea weeds
and patient as a weaver in haute-lisse tapestry,
a Rivera or a Picasso,
with camel-hair alchemy,
paints in *fresco-buono*
the seven panels of a man's tridimensionality
in variforms and varicolors—
since virtue has no Kelvin scale,
since a mother breeds
no twins alike,
since no man is an escape running wild from
self-sown seeds—
then, no man
judged by his biosocial identity

> *in toto*
> can be
> a Kiefekil or a Tartufe,
> an Iscariot or an Iago."

INTERVIEWER: In other words, Dr. Nkomo contends that only in art can one, through the selectivity of the artist, know a character in the round.

TOLSON: Exactly. Socrates' "Know thyself" stated an impossibility. The Old Gadfly meant that one must know one's culture in order to know oneself. Of course, this complicates things, makes it more difficult to know oneself or any other self *in toto*. The artist is the only total *knower*. And yet, even his omniscience concerning a character he himself created may be questioned. Not even Shakespeare escapes this dilemma. Observe the centuries-old, many-angled interpretation of Hamlet, and the sound of fury of controversy through the ages.

INTERVIEWER: You said somewhere that a writer does not write in a vacuum, nor out of a vacuum.

TOLSON: "No man is an escape (that is, a plant) running wild from self-sown seeds." Those words are Dr. Nkomo's.

INTERVIEWER: This seems to make you an environmentalist instead of a hereditist.

TOLSON: How can a Negro be anything else, unless he becomes an "Uncle Tom" or an Iscariot? I repeat: A man is a jack-in-the-box. In International Law, the State is a personality. In the United Nations Assembly there are one hundred and fourteen personalities from every nationality, class, and creed. Every State, therefore, says to its fellow State, "What *manner* of man is this?"

INTERVIEWER: This is quite an intriguing observation. Then, you mean to say that the cause of so much misunderstanding in the United Nations is the fact that the States are in reality ethnic and national persons, with all their diversities?

TOLSON: Certainly. The personalities in the United Nations Assembly need a galaxy of novelists, poets and dramatists to help the diplomats interpret the motivations and actions of all these alien characters.

INTERVIEWER: You disagree with Plato, then, who would banish poets from his Republic.

TOLSON: Yes—although Plato was himself a poet and, therefore, would have banished himself from his own Republic. Perhaps poets are not Shelley's unacknowledged legislators; but, anytime poets are persecuted and even exiled from their society, a ruler has placed a seal on his own oblivion. Do you ask for examples? Well, consider Hitler and Khrushchev. The poet is not only the purifier of language, as Eliot insists, but the poet is a sort of barometer in his society. The Latin word for *poet* is "seer," a "prophet." The Hebrews seemed to have the same idea in the Old Testament, as we see in the Psalms of David and the Songs of Solomon. Through the eyes of Jouve's protagonist in *The Resurrection of the Dead,* the poet foresaw "The White Horse, the Red Horse, the Black Horse, and the fourth Horse, which was the worst." Through the eyes of Markham's protagonist in "The Man with the Hoe," the poet foresaw the earthshaking revolutions that followed the First World War and the Second. Walt Whitman was a seer; Hart Crane, also.

INTERVIEWER: Your name has been bracketed with both. In the Second Section of the *Libretto,* you have The Good Gray Bard in Timbuktu foresee the destruction of those great African empires on the West Coast. Why not read that passage for us?

TOLSON:

> The Good Gray Bard in Timbuktu chanted:
> "Europe is an empty python in hiding grass!"
>
> *Lia! Lia!* The river Wagadu, the river Bagana,
> Became dusty metaphors where white ants ate canoes,
> And the locust Portuguese raped the maiden crops,
> And the sirocco Spaniard razed the city-states,
> And the leopard Saracen bolted his scimitar into
> The jugular vein of Timbuktu. *Dieu seul est grand!*
>
> And now the hyenas whine among the barren bones
> Of the seventeen sun sultans of Songhai,
> And hooded cobras, hoodless mambas, hiss
> In the gold caverns of Falémé and Bambuk,
> And puff adders, hook scorpions, whisper
> In the weedy corridors of Sankoré. *Lia! Lia!*
>
> The Good Gray Bard chants no longer in Timbuktu:
> "The maggots fat on yeas and nays of nut empires!"

INTERVIEWER: I think the two lines,

> And now the hyenas whine among the barren bones
> Of the seventeen sun sultans of Songhai . . .

are magnificent! We seldom see such alliteration and assonance combined. They are symphonic.

TOLSON: I like the synchronization of sight, sound and sense in poetry. I believe I have turned the trick in *Harlem Gallery.* I call these the S-Trinity of Parnassus.

INTERVIEWER: Let us return to the idea of the seer. In the last section of the *Libretto,* you predicted the rise of African republics. You foresaw, as Tennyson before you, a Parliament of Man.

TOLSON: That has been by-passed by many a critic. In 1947, when I was elected Poet Laureate of Liberia, there were only two independent black countries in Africa. Today there are thirty-three. It is a vision, right out of the Apocalypse.

INTERVIEWER: The *New York Times Book Review* said that your *Libretto* pictured not only the historic destiny of the Negro but that of the human race as a whole. A while ago we spoke of the musicality of your poetry. But there is another art that your work suggests to me.

TOLSON: Did you say, "Another art"?

INTERVIEWER: Yes, the art of painting. You have few rivals as a poet in imagistic ability—pictorial power.

TOLSON: You arouse painful memories of my salad days in Missouri. I started out as a boy artist. My father was a minister, poor as the proverbial church mouse in everything but books. Our table suffered because of this insatiable hunger. I was painting pictures when I was three or four years old—to the amazement of the elders. I guess I was pretty good at landscapes and seascapes, street scenes and faces. By the time I was ten, I was framing and peddling my pictures and making big money for a little black boy. I parted my hair in the middle, wore a flowing Windsor tie, and puzzled the elders with words. At twelve, Claude, a lad who was a mulatto prodigy, and I had our own tent show. He could versify anything and invent mechanical toys. I painted the scenery in the tent show and played Caesar to Claude's Macduff. The kids paid their pennies to Claude, the business manager. Sometimes he came up short, because of his interest in girls. When I came across the word "satyr" in my reading, I knew Claude was a prodigy in another sense. Then one day in my twelfth year, at Slater, Missouri, fate entered my life, in strikingly Hardyesque fashion. The church and the parsonage were across from the old Chicago & Alton tracks. I remember that there was a big roundhouse in Slater at that time. One afternoon, a crack train had a "hot-box" across the road and down the embankment from our house. I was in the yard painting a picture. I don't know whether it was Coleridge's "Inspiration" or Cocteau's "Expiration." Anyway, I forgot about the stalled express train and was in the middle of my artwork when I felt, yes, sensed something behind me. I turned suddenly and there stood, leaning on the fence, the very artist I had seen in my art books. He had bushy hair and a magnificent beard. He wore a Byronic collar, an artist's jacket, and an artist's beret. His eyes fixed on mine, he said in Frenchified English, with a grandiloquent florish: "Marvelous! Marvelous! You must go to Paris with me! Where is your father?"

At last my dream had come true! As I ran to the house, I could see in my mind's eye the studios and cafés on the Left Bank of the Seine. I blurted out the good news. My mother stood aghast for a moment. Then she parted the curtains and took an angry look at the bizarre figure leaning on the fence. Suddenly she began to lock every door in the house. As she raced from room to room, she said not a word. That was just like my mother —part Negro and part Indian. After that boyhood tragedy, I never painted another picture. For days and days and days, I brooded. Now, my mother was always making up verses in her head. She was highly intelligent and imaginative, but had little formal education. Like my father, I was a bookworm. Later, much later, I began scribbling verses on tablets and scraps of paper. I repeated, over and over and over, Shakespeare's immortal words in Sonnet 50:

> Not marble, nor the gilded monuments
> Of princes, shall outlive this powerful rhyme.

So, at twelve, I decided to join the immortal poets in a future Paradise.

INTERVIEWER: Is your frustration as a painter the reason for the existence of the *Harlem Gallery,* with its verbal pictures?

TOLSON: A psychiatrist would have to answer that question. I do know that a picture gallery magnetizes me with a potent fascination. Sometimes I have a strange urge to seize a brush, but I have never succumbed to this inner pull of the ego.

INTERVIEWER: Then, what was the genesis of the *Harlem Gallery*—this human comedy with its Balzacian range of characters?

TOLSON: In 1930 I was a student, on a Rockefeller Fellowship, at Columbia University. I met there a dreamer from the University of Iowa, who was trying to put together a Proustian novel. The thesis for my degree was called "The Harlem Group of Negro Writers." As you know, the Twenties gave birth not only to the Lost Generation but to the Harlem Renaissance and the New Negro. Jazz became a fad—ancient African art, a novelty of the intelligentsia. I was in the middle of this literary revolution before the panic of 1929. One day I showed my young white friend a sonnet that I had written. It was titled "Harlem." He read it two or three times, and then said fretfully, "Melvin, Harlem is too big for a sonnet." That was the genesis of the *Harlem Gallery.*

INTERVIEWER: But that was in 1930—thirty-five years ago.

TOLSON: I know it seems like an age. The first finished manuscript of the *Harlem Gallery* was written in free verse. That was the fashion introduced by the Imagists. It contained 340 pages. The *Spoon River Anthology* of Edgar Lee Masters was my model. Browning's psychology in characterization stimulated me. I had deserted the great Romantics and Victorians. Walt Whitman's exuberance was in the marrow of my bones. I peddled the manuscript in the New York market. Nobody wanted it. The publishers and critics said for commercial reasons. A few of the poems appeared in V. F. Calverton's *Modern Quarterly*. Then I stashed the manuscript in my trunk for twenty years. At the end of that time I had read and absorbed the techniques of Eliot, Pound, Yeats, Baudelaire, Pasternak and, I believe, all the great Moderns. God only knows how many "little magazines" I studied, and how much textual analysis of the New Critics. To make a long story short, the new *Harlem Gallery* was completed, and now it is published.

INTERVIEWER: Who are some of the characters in this latest work of art?

TOLSON: To me they are living people, elbowing their varied ways through the chambers of my memory and imagination—lowbrows, middlebrows and highbrows like Dr. Nkomo, the Bantu expatriate and Africanist; Hideho Heights, the Redskin beatnik bard of Lenox Avenue in Harlem; Mr. Guy Delaporte III, the "big shot" of Bola Boa Enterprises, Inc.; Black Orchid, his blues-singing, striptease mistress of the Bamboo Kraal; Dr. Igor Shears, the stoic West Indian patron of the Harlem Symphony Orchestra; Snakehips Briskie, the forefather of the twisters; John Laugart, the half-blind artist from the Harlem catacombs; Kilroy, the president of Afro-American Freedom, Inc.; Black Diamond, the kingpin of the Harlem rackets; the Zulu Club Wits, the Bohemian eggheads of the twilight zone of Afro-American culture.

INTERVIEWER: The *Harlem Gallery* is indeed a cosmopolitan gallery in the human comedy. What character is your favorite?

TOLSON: This is like asking a loving mother to name her favorite child, after she has suffered the doubts and fears of bringing her progeny into the world.

# Robert Hayden's Use of History

## by Charles T. Davis

History has haunted Robert Hayden from the beginning of his career as a poet. In 1941, when a graduate student at the University of Michigan, he worked on a series of poems dealing with slavery and the Civil War called *The Black Spear,* the manuscript which was to win for him a second Hopwood Award.[1] This effort was no juvenile excursion, to be forgotten in the years of maturity. Though some of the poems have not been reprinted in *Selected Poems* (1966),[2] *The Black Spear* survives in a severely altered form in Section Five of that volume. What remains is not simply "O Daedalus, Fly Away Home" and "Frederick Douglass," but a pre-occupation with a continuing historical ambition. This was the desire to record accurately the yearnings, the frustrations, and the achievement of an enslaved but undestroyed people. "Middle Passage," "The Ballad of Nat Turner," and "Runagate, Runagate," all written later, share this concern. In these poems noble Blacks, Cinquez, Nat Turner, and Harriet Tubman, rise from oppression and obscurity.

An extended period of study and research, as well as correspondence in theme, links these later poems with *The Black Spear.* Hayden had intended "Middle Passage" to be the opening work

[1] Robert Hayden discusses the genesis of *The Black Spear* in the third section of a series of exchanges with his editor Paul McCluskey recorded in New York in January, 1971. The whole series was subsequently published in five sections in *How I Write/1* (New York: Harcourt Brace Jovanovich, Inc., 1972). Hayden is one of three literary artists discussed in the book; the others are Judson Philips and Lawson Carter. The third section, "The Black Spear," of "Robert Hayden—The Poet and His Art: A Conversation" is to be found on p. 169–93.

[2] *Selected Poems* (New York: October House Inc., 1966). Subsequent references to *The Black Spear* poems and other early poems will be to this volume.

Robert Hayden's Use of History                                                97

of *The Black Spear,* but the poems in 1941 would not assume a
shape that would satisfy a meticulous craftsman.[3] "The Ballad of
Nat Turner" and "Runagate, Runagate," come from poring over
journals, notebooks, narratives, and histories dealing with the slave
trade, plantation life, slave revolts, and the Underground Railroad,
reading began about 1940 and continued for perhaps a decade,
judging from his recollection of the activity of composition.[4]

A generation later Hayden displays an attachment somewhat less
strong to historical themes. In 1966 "Frederick Douglass" closed
Section Five of *Selected Poems* and the book, a sign of a surviving
commitment. "El-Hajj Malik El-Shabazz (Malcolm X)" opens Section Three "Words in the Mourning Time" of Hayden's most recent
book of poems, bearing the title of the section and published in
1970.[5] Though the commitment to interpreting history is still present, the emphasis has changed. The poems of *The Black Spear*
emerge from the suffering of Black people before Emancipation and
record their assertion of manhood, more than the simple ability to
survive, but those in "Words in the Mourning Time" describe the
agony undergone by Malcolm and others to achieve spiritual
liberation in our own day and the search for meaning in history
upon which that liberation depends. What has endured through the
years is the central importance of history in Hayden's poetry—not
history as the poet would like it to be, but history as he has discovered it.

The birth of the historical impulse in Hayden is not easily described. He seems to have nourished always a sense of the past.
Hayden said in conversation with Paul McCluskey, his editor at
Harcourt Brace Jovanovich: "For some reason, I don't know why,
I seemed to have a need to recall my past and to rid myself of the
pain of so much of it."[6] The poet, then, was discussing poems
written in the 1950's, but the statement applies with equal force to
his work at any stage in his career. The activity of truth-telling from
memory, of reconstructing the past, is purgative—at least, in part,
and it is intimately connected with the necessity to write poems.

[3] *How I Write/1,* p. 175.
[4] *Ibid.,* pp. 175–80.
[5] *Words in the Mourning Time* (New York: October House Inc., 1970). Subsequent references to "El-Hajj Malik El-Shabazz" and other late poems will be to
this volume.
[6] *How I Write/1,* p. 143.

Hayden's predisposition acquired quite early a formal reinforcement. The record of this is bound up with the writing of the poems in *The Black Spear*. Though W. H. Auden, his mentor at Michigan, looked on when Hayden received a prize for *The Black Spear*, the British poet was not the dominant influence shaping the work. That, rather, was Stephen Vincent Benét, whose long historical narrative *John Brown's Body* (1927) moved Hayden to think of approaching slavery and the Civil War "from the black man's point of view." [7] Indeed, Hayden has acknowledged the fact that the title of his sequence of historical poems, *The Black Spear*, comes from Benét and has pointed to a passage appearing late in *John Brown's Body*,[8] in which the reaction of the newly emancipated slaves to Sherman's march through Georgia is described. Benét, in it, commented upon his failure to register in verse the full range and depth of the Black response to the trauma of freedom:

> Oh, black skinned epic, epic with the black spear,
> I cannot sing you, having too white a heart,
> And yet, some day, a poet will rise to sing you
> And sing you with such truth and mellowness,
>
> *        *        *
>
> That you will be a match for any song
> Sung by old, populous nations in the past, . . . (p. 308)

Hayden aspired to become the poet called for by Benét, one with a heart sufficiently Black. Indeed, he told Benét, several years after reading *John Brown's Body* and a year or so before the commencement of serious work on *The Black Spear,* that he intended to write a poem on the materials pointed to by the white poet,[9] though possibly not the "blackskinned epic" so solemnly predicted.

Benét was a hindrance as well as a help, as every major influence must be for a poet struggling to find his own voice. The story of the writing of "Middle Passage" documents the point. This poem, in many ways the most impressive achievement of Hayden's early career, was completed in some form by the time that *The Black Spear* was submitted to the Hopwood judges. But Hayden refused to

---

[7] *Ibid.*, p. 170.
[8] Stephen Vincent Benét, *John Brown's Body* (New York: Farrar and Rinehart, Inc., 1927). Subsequent references to this poem will be to this edition.
[9] *How I Write/1*, p. 170.

include it in his volume, despite the fact that he had planned it as the inaugural piece of the whole sequence. And his reasons for delay are good ones: "Actually I had tried writing the poem in blank verse—unrhymed iambic pentameter—but, then, it was too much like Benét, not only in form, but in diction and narrative organization also." [10] The statement prepares us for differences in the final form of the poem, published originally in *Phylon* in 1945,[11] but it also requires us to look for correspondences with *John Brown's Body*, because Benét's influence has been so powerful and pervasive.

The section of *John Brown's Body* which is closest to Hayden's "Middle Passage" is the one that appears immediately after the "invocation," "Prelude—the Slaver." [12] Benét presents here the captain of a slave ship who is moved to comment on a profession in which he is skilled, while actually transporting a cargo of black ivory from Africa to America. The impulse toward self-revelation is aroused by the questions, often not stated but implied, posed by a young mate, who is inexperienced and innocent. The bulk of the narrative consists of exchanges between the two. The Captain is firm in his piety: he reads his Bible regularly and sees no contradiction between practicing Christianity and ferrying for profit Blacks to a life of enforced and unending servitude. The Mate is less certain; he recoils from what he sees—the Blacks in chains, the threat of the plague, the hatred of the enslaved, and he yearns for his and the Captain's native New England. Most of all, he is upset by what he calls the Blackness, the stench that is everywhere, the stain that will not wash out. His own emotions approach a mystical terror that seems to deny the Captain's pieties, a terror more appropriate for the sinning than for those who take comfort in the fact that they are adding heathen Black souls to Christ's kingdom.

Hayden takes over the problem of reconciling Christianity and slavetrading in "Middle Passage," [13] though the machinery of his narrative is much more complicated. The first of three parts offers the log entries, the prayers, and the ruminations of a pious member

---

[10] *Ibid.*, p. 176.
[11] "Middle Passage," *Phylon*, VI (Third Quarter, 1945), pp. 247–53. The poem was revised and shortened by the omission of an introductory section before republication in *Selected Poems*.
[12] *John Brown's Body*, pp. 8–13.
[13] *Selected Poems*, pp. 67–70.

of the crew of a slaver. The conflict, however, is internal rather than external. The spur toward self-revelation is not an innocent youth on a maiden voyage, but the consciousness of the speaker, as he feels the threat to body and soul in the hazards and the emotional excesses that come from participation in the slave trade. Once again we find Black resistance, rebellion and implacable hatred, and the threat of the plague. To these familiar difficulties, Hayden adds a new trial—the temptation to lust with Black wenches, the giving up wholly to sex and alcohol so that ship, slaves, and self are all lost.

Hayden's addition points to one of the differences separating Benét's poem from his own—the richness of his documentation. The accurate touches that come from Hayden's wide reading are impressive. His wealth of information is to be seen in Part One in the names of the slave ships, the form of the ship's log, the description of the creeping blindness (Ophthalmia), and the graphic account of the drunken orgy aboard *The Bella J.* Parts Two and Three, almost untouched by the example of Benét's poem, display evidences of extensive research in the slave trade in the library of the University of Michigan.[14] The recollections of the bluff slave trader, undistorted by qualms of conscience, describe the slave factories, the collection methods, the corruption of Black kings, and the good times on the West African coast. Following this straightforward statement, we hear in Part Three the testimony of a Spanish slaver, who supplies from his own point of view the details of the *Amistad* Mutiny in 1839. Now, the sources of Hayden's knowledge are many, but he recalls two as being especially rewarding, *Adventures of an African Slaver*[15] and Muriel Rukeyser's biography *Willard Gibbs,*[16] which presents an accurate description of the *Amistad* Mutiny and the trial that followed.

Though Benét's poem might have suggested to Hayden the technique of handling the poetic problems of "Middle Passage" through the use of voices, it could not provide a model for the subtle use of the technique which Hayden's poem displays. Benét's "Prelude" has three voices—the skipper's, the mate's, and the poet's. Actually the

[14] *How I Write/1*, p. 175.
[15] Brantz Mayer, *Adventures of an African Slaver* (New York: A. and C. Boni, 1928).
[16] Muriel Rukeyser, *Willard Gibbs* (Garden City, N.Y.: Doubleday, Doran and Co., 1942).

poet intrudes very little, only to utter prophecy in a brief section toward the end of the poem. According to the poet, the black seeds "robbed from a black king's storehouse" (p. 12) would fall on American earth, "lie silent, quicken" (p. 12) and then grow. A seed would become "A black shadow-sapling, a tree of shadow," and the tree, the poet promises, would ultimately blot out "all the seamen's stars" (p. 12). An ominous prediction, then, is offered, one that identifies the shaking of the leaves of the shadow tree with the trampling of the "horses of anger," the "Beat of the heavy hooves like metal on metal," (p. 12), the signs of war. The poet of the "Prelude" engages, then, in the necessary prefiguration of the Civil War that he will describe in later books.

The poet of "Middle Passage" has a good deal more to do. His is the central consciousness of the poem, providing a frame in Part One for the description of the painful voyage from Africa to America and, at the beginning of the poem, extracting meaning for the journey: "voyage through death to life upon these shores" (p. 65). A crew member of a slave ship provides the actual description of the Middle Passage itself. His narration is not simple because it is made complex by the fact of his piety. On the one hand, there is the sailor's prosaic voice, instructing us in entries in ship's logs and, finally, in a legal deposition, of the hazards of a rebellious cargo, disease, and lust. On the other hand, there is the voice praying for "safe passage" to bring "heathen souls" to God's "chastening" (p. 65). What the sailor tells has so much cruelty and depravity that it seems finally to overwhelm the teller of the tale. The secure sense of accomplishing God's design departs, and there is only the cry, despairing, now, rather than confident: "Pilot Oh Pilot Me" (p. 67).

The poet echoes, clearly, the cry of the sailor. He has been moved deeply by the prosaic account in rather different ways. For one thing, he is aware of the irony present in the crew man's piety, and he comments, in the language of Shakespeare's Ariel and with a precedent provided by *The Waste Land*:[17]

---

[17] Ariel's famous song in *The Tempest* begins:

> Full fathom five thy father lies,
>   Of his bones are coral made,
> Those are pearls that were his eyes,
>   Nothing of him that doth fade

> Deep in the festering hold thy father lies,
> of his bones New England pews are made,
> those are altar lights that were his eyes (p. 65).

The allusion to Shakespeare's sea-change mocks a less spiritual transformation, though Hayden's too has a claim to religious motivation. The "altar lights" in a church in New England are vulgar consequences of an investment in Black gold. Moreover, the poet speculates quite openly on the destiny of the Yankee slave ship, with the benefit of a greater perspective and more knowledge than the sailor:

> What port awaits us, Davy Jones'
> or home? I've heard of slavers drifting, drifting,
> playthings of wind and storm and chance, their crews
> gone blind, the jungle hatred
> crawling up on deck (p. 66).

The poet's historical perspective appears more clearly in subsequent parts. In Part Two the poet becomes the "lad," who listens to the recollections of a hardened and unrepentant slaver, reconstructing the beginnings of the wretched trade in Africa in greed, vanity, war, deception, devastation, and disease. In Part Three the historical perspective acquires an important spiritual dimension. Here the slave ships become "shuttles in the rocking loom of history" (p. 68) and the pattern from the loom itself emerges. The ships, though they may bear "bright ironical names like 'Jesus', 'Estrella', 'Esperanza', 'Mercy' " (p. 65), contribute to "New World littorals that are / mirage and myth and actual shore" (p. 68). The poet promises the "actual shore," and the journey to it, the middle passage, becomes a descent into death resembling the dark night of the soul. The "shore" is life at the end of death, but first Blacks must experience death, a "voyage whose chartings are unlove" (p. 68).

Cinquez, the leader of the *Amistad* Mutiny, assumes especial

---

> But doth suffer a sea-change
> Into something rich and strange                    (Iii 397–402).

One reference in *The Waste Land* (T. S. Eliot, *The Complete Poems and Plays,* 1909–1950 [New York: Harcourt, Brace and World, Inc., 1952]) appears in Part II, "A Game of Chess" (p. 41):

> I remember
> Those are pearls that were his eyes                (II 124–25).

prominence in the poet-speaker's vision of "Middle Passage." The Spanish slaver considers Cinquez "that surly brute who calls himself a prince, / directing, urging on the ghastly work" (p. 69). But in the enlightened historical perspective of the poet, Cinquez is an expression of "The deep immortal human wish, / the timeless will," (p. 70). He is seen as an early sign of "life upon these shores," a "deathless primaveral image, / life that transfigures many lives" (p. 70). Hayden describes, then, a second sea-change, one more genuine than the transformation of the "festering hold" into pews and altar lights in New England because this change transfigures Blacks. Cinquez, on the bloody deck of the *Amistad* and beyond the "butchered bodies" (p. 69) of the slave crew, points to the discovery of manhood and human dignity, even to recognition by law (thanks to "the august John Quincy Adams," p. 70).

Nothing resembling this historical vision appears in *John Brown's Body*. Benét sees the Civil War as the "pastoral rebellion of the earth / Against machines, against the Age of Steam" (p. 334), and out of John Brown's body grows "the new, mechanic birth, / . . . the great, metallic Beast / Expanding West and East" (p. 335). Hayden is not concerned with these problems, but rather with the transformation of slave to man, a transfiguration frequently touched with mystical overtones in his poems.

All of the poems of Section Five of *Selected Poems* have this preoccupation of Hayden's. Nat Turner in the darkness of the Dismal Swamp has a vision of bright angels in fiery combat, and he rises from his dream "at last free / And purified, . . ." (p. 74), and committed to holy war. He knows, then, that the "conqueror faces" (p. 73), of his dream were like his. Harriet Tubman, in "Runagate, Runagate," rises above the impulsive, headlong flight of slaves to the North to insert steel in the spines of the timid, to provide light and direction to the bewildered, and threaten death to the faltering and craven. She is "woman of earth, whipscarred, / a summoning, a shining" (p. 76), asserting a single objective, "Mean to be free" (p. 76). Indeed, only she, "alias The General / alias Moses Stealer of Slaves" (p. 76), knows that one must be "mean" to be free. The spiritual justification of her purpose comes in lines echoing the language of a Negro spiritual toward the conclusion of the poem:

> Midnight Special on a sabre track movering movering,
> first stop Mercy and the last Hallelujah

Though the mystical transformation of the desire to be free, to assert manhood, links all of Hayden's historical poems of this period, "The Ballad of Nat Turner" and "Runagate, Runagate" point to the importance for Hayden of another kind of source material. Behind these poems, indeed, lies the research of the 1940's that supported "Middle Passage" as well, an accumulation of materials so rich that Hayden was moved to write a play about Harriet Tubman, *Go Down, Moses.*[18] He recalls, in reviewing formal sources, that *The Negro in Virginia,* a study completed in 1940 by the Writer's Program of the Work Projects Administration and supervised by Roscoe E. Lewis of Hampton Institute,[19] had especial value for him as he prepared to write "The Ballad of Nat Turner." But this familiar pattern of research and rumination received support from a knowledge of a type of source material not found in "Middle Passage." This was the Negro folk tradition.

Nat Turner is struck by the cessation in the turning of the wheel within a wheel, an image that recalls the spiritual celebrating Ezekiel's illumination. The details of the celestial combat have the vividness and the primitive power of a folk sermon. Nat's account in a moment of intense excitement tends to employ the repetition found so frequently in the words of a folk preacher, suggesting with its incantatory rhythms the chant that accompanies traditionally God's direct influence upon his mortal instrument:

> But I saw I saw oh many of
>    those mighty beings waver.
> Waver and fall, go streaking down
>    into swamp water, and the water
> hissed and steamed and bubbled and locked
>    shuddering shuddering over (p. 73).

There is a folk basis too for the references to Africa, for those intimations of the mother land that come to Blacks frequently in darkness and in the forest:

> where Ibo warriors
> hung shadowless, turning in wind
> that moaned like Africa (p. 72).

---

[18] *How I Write/1*, p. 188.
[19] *The Negro in Virginia* (New York: Hastings House, Publishers, 1940).

"Runagate, Runagate" has linguistic touches that suggest a strong folk inspiration, with "jack-muh-lanterns" (p. 75), "patterol-lers" (p. 76), an "a-murbling" (p. 76) fear, a "movering" (p. 77) train, "jaybird-talk" (p. 76) and "oh Susyanna" (p. 76). The invitation to get aboard the coach to the North is extended to enslaved Blacks in accents that show dialect roots:

> Come ride–a my train
> Mean mean mean to be free (p. 77).

The language is just a sign of the rich reliance upon the materials that come ultimately from the folk imagination. We have the vision of the free North as the "star-shaped yonder Bible city" (p. 75), the association of the journey to freedom with the "North star and bonanza gold" (p. 76), the identification of the flight itself as "crossing over" (p. 75) or as the freedom train, and the assumed connection between the calling of the hoot-owl and the "hants in the air" (p. 77). Not the least of these evidences of the pressure of folk culture intimately known are the snatches from the spirituals. Though these are mostly echoes rather than direct quotations, there are two lines, indeed, that come without change from the great spiritual that begins with the phrase "Oh-h freedom":

> And before I'll be a slave
> I'll be buried in my grave.

Hayden relies upon folk materials almost exclusively in only one poem in Section V of *Selected Poems*—"O Daedalus, Fly Away Home." Like the others, this poem transforms mystically the desire for freedom. In an interview with Paul McCluskey, Hayden has identified the source of the poem as "a legend common among the Georgia Sea Island Negroes—the legend of the Flying African." [20] He adds that it was their belief that certain slaves had the magical power to fly to freedom in Africa. The poetic machinery that supports this central idea uses other elements in a folk culture. The metrics of the poem suggest the rhythm of a folk dance called "juba," widely performed by slaves in the antebellum South. The instruments providing the musical background are a "coonskin drum" and a "jubilee banjo" (p. 71). The only touch in the poem that does not show the influence of Negro folk history is the refer-

---

[20] *How I Write/1*, p. 180.

ence to Daedalus in the title and the resonance that is achieved
throughout from the comparison with an earlier and better known
historical flight.

History, formal and folk, serves Hayden's purpose, and that purpose in the early historical poems is to describe the mystical emergence of freedom from circumstances that appall and degrade, and
the making of a man, a Black man in America. No better description of the poet's objective exists than the first lines of the justly
famous tribute to Frederick Douglass:

> When it is finally ours, this freedom, this liberty, this
>      beautiful
> and terrible thing, needful to man as air,
>      usable as earth; . . . (p. 78).

Contributing to Douglass's eminence is his own "middle passage,"
his painful exposure to death in various forms—physical violence,
humiliation, and ostracism:

> this man, this Douglass, this former slave, this Negro
> beaten to his knees, exiled, visioning a world
> where none is lonely, none hunted, alien, . . . (p. 78).

Following death comes life, not simply for Douglass, whose image
survives in our memories, but for us all. In a voice touched with
awe at the transformation, the poet concludes his tribute in this way:

> Oh, not with statues' rhetoric,
> not with legends and poems and wreaths of bronze alone,
> but with the lives grown out of his life, the lives
> fleshing his dream of the beautiful, needful thing (p. 78).

The end of the Douglass sonnet echoes, then, the theme of "Middle
Passage":

> Voyage through death
>      to life upon these shores

and offers again the great theme of the historical poems of Hayden's
early period.

Hayden's poems published in 1970, *Words in the Mourning Time,*
reveal a persistence of an interest in historical materials, but they
do not have the focus or the concentration which the ideal of *The
Black Spear* provided. No doubt, the poet's own soul has yielded to

"migratory habits" (p. 64),[21] which the poet represents as being the theme of Socrates at his "hemlock hour." Like Socrates, Hayden faces a world not entirely reassuring to the firmness of his early vision. The startling carcasses, "death's black droppings" (p. 64), strewn about the Fisk University lawns are bad enough, but they suggest, with their troublesome presence, the existence of more serious challenges elsewhere.

The consequence of "middle passage" are not all good, nor all life. The poet travels to Lookout Mountain,[22] the site of a great Civil War battle, where the agony of suffering, struggle, and death was most acute, and finds himself among "Sunday alpinists" who "pick views and souvenirs" (p. 26). The Union victory seems "dubious," to say the least, when from the perspective of "A world away," the poet is moved to say:

> . . . the scions of that fighting climb
> endless hills of war, amid war's peaks
> and valleys broken, scattered fall (p. 26).

The Roman rhetoric heard at the *Amistad* trial in "Middle Passage" has become the song of the "stuffed gold eagle" (p. 26).

Confusion comes from something other than the failure of the time to live up to its brightest vision; it occurs in the minds of those who stand to benefit most from the realization of the dream —the oppressed Blacks. Hayden's dramatic poem "The Dream" deals with this problem. Old Sinda remains behind in the slave quarters after "Marse Lincum's soldier boys" (p. 12) had brought freedom to the plantation. This "ragged jubilo" (p. 12) did not

---

[21] In "A Plague of Starlings." The poem has this final stanza:

> And if not careful
> I shall tread
> upon carcasses
> carcasses when I
> go morning now
> to lecture on
> what Socrates,
> the hemlock hour nigh,
> told sorrowing
> Phaedo and the rest
> about the migratory
> habits of the soul (p. 64).

[22] "On Lookout Mountain" (p. 26).

accord with Sinda's expectations, and she hid in the quarters rather than follow, rejoicing, in the wake of the army. Her dream of emancipation is infinitely more attractive, and Sinda sees the faces of her sons Cal and Joe, and that of Charlie, possibly their father, who was sold to the ricefields many years before, on "the great big soldiers marching out of gunburst" and she will not accept "those Buckcras with their ornery / funning cussed commands" (p. 12). These were not "the hosts the dream had promised her" (p. 12). Sinda fails to understand that war is prose, recorded in Cal's letters to her about the "Kernul" and the "contrybans," the rain, the hard-tack and the bullybeef, the "ficety gals," and the constant worry about the "Bullit" with his name "rote on it." And liberation is prose too. But Sinda will cling to her vision until she dies, until the very end of her waning, "brittle strength" (p. 13).

"On Lookout Mountain" and "The Dream" are comments on history that have especial value in light of *The Black Spear,* since they deal with the pain and the expectation attached to the Civil War, but they do not confront directly the problems of recent history. "El-Hajj Malik El-Shabazz (Malcolm X)" does this. Certain prefigurations come from "On Lookout Mountain" and "The Dream" that prepare us for Hayden's approach to the career of Malcolm X. One is the poet's objection to the vulgar and material-istic limitations in contemporary American culture; another is the poet's sense of the possibility of distortion, even corruption, in the mind of the holder of the dream. Both are related to the epigraph of "El-Hajj Malik El-Shabazz": "O masks and metamorphoses of Ahab, Native Son" (p. 37).

Malcolm, like Douglass, is a folk hero. What is required to measure the man is an understanding of the folk milieu out of which he came as well as his position in history as a charismatic leader of Black people. The two kinds of historical knowledge which Hayden displayed in "The Ballad of Nat Turner" and in "Runa-gate, Runagate" are present here as well. The folk mores that rest behind Malcolm's emergence are urban, however, not rural. No doubt, the poet's memory of his own childhood in black Detroit gives especial poignancy to the reconstruction of Malcolm's early years. There is no question about the authority of his description of "Dee-troit Red" on the street:

> He conked his hair and Lindy-hopped,
> zoot-suited jiver, swinging those chicks
> in the hot rose and reefer glow (p. 37).

Hayden is equally prepared to face the thorny problem of Malcolm's place in history. His consideration must begin with Malcolm's sense of his role, with the facts of the *Autobiography*.[23] The reliance seems to be especially clear when the poet refers to the tragic end of Malcolm's father and mother, to his reputation in prison ("'Satan' in The Hole" [p. 38]), and to his intimations of his own violent death. But Hayden moves beyond the *Autobiography* to comment on Malcolm's Black Muslim faith. What stirs the poet is something other than a casual interest in Islam; it is the concern of a man deeply touched by the power of an Eastern religion, a devoted Bahaist who can sympathize with a conversion to a faith that many think exotic. Personal factors as well as the passion for accuracy combine to describe the historical phenomenon that is Malcolm.

The documentation of Malcolm's commitment to Islam has impressive economy. Important to his faith is the narrative attributed to Elijah Muhammad, the leader of the Nation of Islam among Black Americans, about the creation of the white man. "Yacub's white-faced treachery" (p. 38) refers to the original mistake in genetic experimentation that led to the ultimate suppression of Blacks by upstart and diabolical whites. In this version of creation there is no doubt about the color, rather the lack of it, of Ahab, the unholy king. Arabic phrases in Hayden's poem are fortunate and functional additions. Something of the evangelical character of the faith and of the excitement that thrills the faithful is conveyed through these exclamations. The poet describes with precision Malcolm's role in the movement:

> He X'd his name, became his people's anger,
> exhorted them to vengeance for their past;
> rebuked, admonished them,
>
> their scourger who
> would shame them, drive them from
> the lush ice gardens of their servitude (p. 59).

[23] Malcolm X, *The Autobiography of Malcolm X* (New York: Grove Press, Inc., 1966).

Malcolm becomes Christ in this passage, angrily driving the money changers from the temple. There is accuracy in this comparison, and there is irony, too, if we consider Christ something other than Calvin's creation, with the "hellward-thrusting hands" (p. 38) that so repelled Malcolm. The irony becomes explicit rather than potential when the poet adds: "Rejecting Ahab, he was of Ahab's tribe" (p. 39).

The presence of ironies ties "El-Hajj Malik El-Shabazz" to "Middle Passage." In the earlier poem the play upon "sea-change" adds dimension to Hayden's statement; in the poem about Malcolm the "dawn" functions in much the same way. A "false dawn of vision" precedes a true awakening. Malcolm is first converted, through the offices of Elijah Muhammad, to a faith in a "racist Allah," one whose "adulterate attars could not cleanse / him of the odors of the pit" (p. 38). His pilgrimage to Mecca sparks a "final metamorphosis," a truer revelation that eliminates hate as a necessary component of faith. Malcolm moves from neo-Islam to orthodox Islam, and Hayden celebrates the second conversion:

> He fell upon his face before
> Allah the raceless in whose blazing Oneness all
> were one. He rose renewed renamed, became
> much more than there was time for him to be (p. 40).

Hayden's tribute to El-Hajj Malik El-Shabazz, formerly Malcolm X, renamed after the Hajj rituals or the rites of the pilgrimage to Mecca, expresses a view of what the movement in history should be. The early poems record Hayden's vision of a Black man who has acquired freedom and humanity. The later poems, dealing with history after Emancipation, describe the confused wanderings and the tormenting frustrations of the liberated man, but they still maintain that modern man must become more human. The first part of the long poem "Words in the Mourning Time," a lament for the deaths of Martin Luther King and Robert Kennedy, sketches this necessary development in our culture, upon which our survival depends. The destruction of King and Kennedy—and of El-Hajj Malik El-Shabazz—represents for us a "middle passage" to "life upon these shores":

> the agonies of our deathbed childbed age
> are process, major means whereby,
> oh dreadfully, our humanness must be achieved (p. 41).

The heroes of history in this time of mourning are different from those in *The Black Spear*. They are more fallible, more vulnerable, more confused, and more easily destroyed, but El-Hajj Malik El-Shabazz matures to share a vision that Douglass has seen and which Hayden still enunciates with eloquence:

> a human world where godliness
> is possible and man
> is neither gook nigger honkey wop nor kike
>
> but man
>
> permitted to be man (p. 49).[24]

[24] The final lines of Part IX in "Words in the Mourning Time."

# Imamu Amiri Baraka:
# The Quest for Moral Order

## by Lee A. Jacobus

LeRoi Jones' poetry describes a quest for a moral order which
he feels ultimately impelled to create for himself and on his own
terms. It begins as a moral order similar to T. S. Eliot's in *The
Waste Land* and similar to the order insisted upon by the comic
books and the radio serials of Jones' youth. The moral order Jones
searched for is related to Eliot's hanged man, who appears frequently
in Jones' work. But it is also related to the hero as something other
than victim: to the existential hero who, like the Shadow, the Lone
Ranger, and Green Lantern, can act individually to impose a strong
moral order on a disordered world. Yet both of these visions are rejected. Of Eliot's Jewish God, he says, "jewchrist, that's hunkie
bread, turned green";[1] the hanged man becomes not God, but a
black, lynched granddaddy;[2] and "THE SHADOW IS DEAD." [3]
All his heroes die; his values are inverted: "We are / in love with
the virtue of evil";[4] his only recourse is to become his own hero in
the streets, to create his own black gods, and to preach a destruction
of the old order as a means of preparing for the new. The pain and
anguish he experienced in reaching this point—including the loss
of faith in the old heroes and the old moral order—are the subject

[1] "Lowdown," *Black Magic* (Indianapolis and New York: Bobbs–Merrill, 1969),
p. 74. Other volumes cited in the text are *Preface to a Twenty Volume Suicide
Note* (New York: Totem Press and Corinth Books, 1961) and *The Dead Lecturer* (New York: Grove Press, Inc., 1964).

[2] "Biography," *Black Magic*, pp. 124–25.

[3] "THREE MOVEMENTS AND A CODA," *Black Magic*, p. 103.

[4] "Red Eye," *Black Magic*, p. 72.

of the bulk of the poems in his three published volumes, *Preface to a Twenty Volume Suicide Note* (1961), *The Dead Lecturer* (1964), and *Black Magic* (1969).

In view of the influences Jones recognizes in his own work, Baudelaire, Duncan, Olson, Ginsberg, to name a few, it may seem strange to isolate Eliot. But Eliot's influence is pervasive: it operates on many levels simultaneously. The fragmented structure of *The Waste Land* figures in many of Jones' more difficult poems, particularly in the poems of the fifties and early sixties. The vision of the world as wasted and infertile; the vision of a world having turned its back on God; the vision of rat's feet through the ruined city all seem as much a part of Jones' poetry as of Eliot's. Rhythms which are decidedly Eliotic crop up in crucial moments in the early—and sometimes the late—poems. And innumerable direct references and allusions to Eliot pepper all the poems, though they are most obvious and most frequent in the middle work. What all this seems to point to is an effort on Jones' part to understand the moral dilemma of his own situation as a black man in a white city, oppressed and displaced in his own land, in the mythic terms which satisfied Eliot and which concerned the ultimate problem of God, moral order, the disregard of man, and the hope of resolution through love and faith. In Eliot we find the thin edge of despair honed to razor sharpness only to be neutralized by faith in a God for whom justice is clear, unambiguous, and thorough—if not sudden and swift.

In a series of three poems called "From an Almanac," in *Preface to a Twenty Volume Suicide Note*, Jones talks about winter winds and words drowned in the wind, words at the mercy of the "clown gods." The connection with Eliot's God is unclear until the second of the Almanac poems, when the hanged man appears:

> Respect the season
> and dance to the rattle
> of its bones.
> > The flesh
> hung
> from trees. Blown
> down. A cold
> music. A colder
> hand, will grip
> you. Your bare

soul. (Where is the soul's place. What is
its
nature?) Winter rattles
like the throat
of the hanged man.

It is almost impossible not to see in this an effort to describe a moral season, the cruelest season in Jones' terms, of nature battering man with cruel winds—with the hanged man himself "Swung / against our windows"!

"From an Almanac (3)" is dedicated, "(For C. O.)," undoubtedly Charles Olson, since the poem is reminiscent of Olson's own work. But the influence is mingled with allusions, not only to Eliot, but to Milton as well. The question is the question of dancing, which interested Duncan and fascinated Olson enough that he wrote a syllabary on it. Jones propounds it, wondering how the children of winter could bring themselves, in this season, to dance at all.

This bizness, of dancing, how
can it suit us? Old men, naked
sterile women.
                    (our time,
a cruel one. Our soul's warmth
left out. Little match children,
dance
against the weather.
                              )The soul's
warmth
is how
shall I say
it,
        Its own. A place
of warmth, for children
wd dance there,
                        if they cd. If they
left their brittle selves behind (our time's
a cruel one.
                    Children
of winter. (I cross myself
like religion
                    Children
of a cruel time. (the wind

> stirs the bones
> & they drag clumsily
> thru the cold.)
>                     These children
> are older
> than their worlds. and
> cannot dance.

If some of these images are reminiscent of *The Waste Land*, the themes are equally reminiscent of *Four Quartets*. The querulousness, the seasons, the children, and the dance are all important in the *Quartets*. But the differences in tone and the apparent loss of hope in Jones' poems are telling of a change. Where Jones talks about "Old men, naked / sterile women" when he asks whether dancing is possible, Eliot sees a vision of a sacrament. Eliot sees dancing specifically as a metaphor for matrimony and "of the coupling of man and woman." He says, "The association of man and woman / In daunsinge, signifying matrimonie— / A dignified and commodious sacrament" ("East Coker," I). And later, in "Little Gidding," II, he says, "From wrong to wrong the exasperated spirit / Proceeds, unless restored by that refining fire / Where you must move in measure, like a dancer." For Jones the season is winter; his children are aged and infertile; and the only source of warmth is the soul, which is "Its own. A place," isolated and by no means a "refining fire." The children cannot dance. Their chances of taking part in "A dignified and commodious sacrament" are slight. They are match children whose refining fire is so slight it can neither refine nor support.

Jones' almanac is a moral almanac, like Eliot's record of the seasons; both their landscapes are moral landscapes, with the wind and the cold not only affecting, but reflecting the souls of men. The differences in their views lie perhaps in the feeling, on Eliot's part, that though the world has been wasted by man, God could somehow still inspirit it if he wished. Eliot's view is that there is a moral order in the nature of things which man has somehow lost the key to. Eliot's view in *The Waste Land* is certainly a despairing one, though the *Four Quartets* demonstrates that his ultimate faith is not shaken. The fact that man has defiled and destroyed is not sufficient grounds for ignoring the original moral order. But for Jones such is not at all so clearly the case. His almanac poems suggest a picture of despair. The winds are cutting, the people infertile, the children impossibly aged. The question of the soul and the question of religion figure strongly in the almanacs as they do in many of the rest of his poems. But Jones has no basic conviction that the basic moral order is there and needs only to be understood anew. Jones in no way renounces his faith in God, but he examines in painful detail his relation to Eliot's God. In these early poems the distinction between Jones' God and Eliot's God seems almost academic. The images Jones uses correspond closely enough to Eliot's to convince us that they are one and the same, the hanged man—Jesus Christ. But the fact seems to be that Jones is examining from the very first the nature of God, that he is trying to see himself in relation to Christ and Eliot's vision, and that he ultimately renounces Eliot's God on the grounds that the moral order is inverted because of the nature of the God himself. If he wishes to set things straight for himself, he must give up the Christian God and find his own.

The way in which the poems document the progression of his thought is remarkable. Jones is careful to tell us that he has put his poems together in as close to chronological order as possible, and consequently we can watch the progression in detail. Each of the following quotes and references will be accompanied by a page reference to the published volumes so that the nature of the progression can be fully appreciated at a glance.

In the first half of *Preface to a Twenty Volume Suicide Note* Jones does not worry himself directly about Eliot's God. He is more concerned with what he calls the "Mosaic of disorder I own but cannot recognize." [5] The word "disorder" appears frequently in the middle of *Preface*: in the musical poem for Billy Holiday called "Bridge"; in "Way Out West," in "the intricate disorder / of the seasons"; and in "The Turncoat," in a mixing of memory and desire: "with dull memories & self hate, & the terrible disorder / of a young man." Of course, self-hatred figures in other poems of this collection and it seems to be connected with disorder. The disorder of the seasons is reflected upon in the Almanac poems and becomes ultimately apocalyptic in "Roi's New Blues" (pp. 45–6) when he offers us an abrupt shift in address in the middle of the poem—recalling "Winter kept us warm"—in "Winter locked us in. (On / the floor, at midnight / we turned in blind / embrace." He says, "Coldness will be /

---

[5] "Vice," *Preface,* p. 28.

stamped out, when those grey horsemen / with sunny faces / ride through our town. O, God / we've waited for them. Stood / for years with our eyes full / of a violent wind." Though they have grey faces—"grey" becomes synonymous with "white" later, just as the sun is sometimes linked with white dominance—they are the horsemen of the apocalypse, and Jones somehow causes himself to feel that they will ride and revenge. They will set right the wrongs.

*The Dead Lecturer* is a more detailed search for God than *Preface*. Jones is more explicit, as if he was taking more seriously the message he himself sends us: "Let my poems be a graph / of me" (p. 10). In "A Poem for Willie Best," Section VII, Jones complains that he is treating of "no God / but what is given. Give me. / Something more / than what is here. I must tell you / my body hurts" (p. 24). His need is clear, his pain is somehow embedded in the pain of Willie Best, an actor like Step'nfetchit whose degradation is shared by Jones. In his search for something more, Jones dredges up several images from *The Waste Land* in the ending of "A Poem for Democrats." The hanged man merges with the Phoenician merchant to share a death by drowning, an ironic mafia-style death with cement overshoes:

> (transporting your loved one
> across the line is death
> by drowning.
> > Drowned love
> hanged man, swung, cement on his feet.)
> > > **But**
> the small filth of the small mind
> short structures of
> newark, baltimore, cincinnati, omaha. **Distress,**
> europe has passed we are alone. Europe
> frail woman, dead, we are alone (p. 39)

The echo of "Jerusalem Athens Alexandria / Vienna London / Unreal" is unmistakable, and the ironies in the poem are not confined to the substitution of these middle-sized cities we now associate with black unrest, if not despair. The chief irony is that the hanged man is drowned in a manner which suggests the mafia—new Romans, doing what old Romans did, but with the modern twist of premixed, quick-drying overshoes.

Jones describes "a wreck of spirit, / a heap of broken feeling," in

"Duncan spoke of a process" (p. 54), and talks of feeling that he must cling to "what futile lies / I have," though he begins to recognize them as lies. Perhaps the beginning of the rejection of Eliot's God most clearly comes in the two "Black Dada Nihilismus" poems. They are remarkable in their clarity—once the trend of Jones' thinking and feeling is seen. What Jones sees is history and the sins committed in the name of Christ. He says, "God, if they bring him / bleeding, I would not / forgive, or even call him / black dada nihilismus" (p. 61). Jones speaks of "the umbrella'd jesus," as if he had mixed him with the image of Gandhi, but he links Jesus with the alchemy of conquest: converting flesh, not to bread, but to wealth:

> Trismegistus, have
>
> them, in their transmutation, from stone
> to bleeding pearl, from lead to burning
> looting, dead Moctezuma, find the West (p. 62)

Then, in the second, and much more brutally forceful poem, Jones speaks almost as if he were nostalgic for a Mau-Mau revolt: "Plastique, we / do not have, only thin heroic blades." Then, "Rape the white girls. Rape / their fathers. Cut the mothers' throats. / Black dada nihilismus, choke my friends." And the poem ends with as clear a call for revenge—or what some call justice—as Jones is capable of at this time:

> art, 'member
> what you said
> money, God, power,
> a moral code, so cruel
> it destroyed Byzantium, Tenochtitlan, Commanch,
>
> > > > > > (got it, *Baby!*
> For tambo, willie best, dubois, patrice, mantan, the
> bronze buckaroos.
>
> > > For Jack Johnson, asbestos, tonto, buckwheat,
> > > billie holiday.
> > > > For tom russ, l'overture, vesey, beau jack,
> (may a lost god damballah, rest or save us
> against the murders we intend
> against his lost white children
> black dada nihilismus (p. 64)

The moral code is "so cruel" (a phrase he uses several times in his early poetry to refer to something which is in him—is it this moral code?) that it destroys not just men or races, but entire empires, whole civilizations. It is no wonder that he renounces it. But he does not renounce God, nor does he seem to slacken his quest:

> Who cannot but yearn
> for the One Mind, or Right, or call it some God, a thing beyond
> themselves, some thing toward which all life is fixed, some static,
> irreducible, constantly correcting, dogmatic economy
> > of the soul.
> ("Green Lantern's Solo," p. 70)

Critics who have seen nihilism and nothing more in these poems and in Jones' work are simply wrong. He is looking for something —for a God and a moral code—which will not destroy empires or him. By no means is he fearful of violence or destruction so long as it produces the destruction of the code that destroyed Moctezuma. He sees no irony in the need for such violence: no more than one sees in the destruction of Sodom and Gomorrah, perhaps a reasonable analogy. In fact, by this time in his work, Jones has revealed himself—through his references to Sartre in the beginning of his second black dada nihilismus poem—as suffering an existential transmutation. He is passing, at the end of *The Dead Lecturer,* through a dark existential night of the soul, out of which an entire reordering must result. He reorders himself in relation to God, his soul, and his morality to begin to accept the existential role of action or of agent.

It is no accident and no irony that "Green Lantern's Solo" is one of the last poems of *The Dead Lecturer* and that it contains the kinds of existential sentiments that it does. Throughout the early work, Jones constantly links his comic book heroes with the search for moral order. Those heroes are not only men of action, but men of understanding: " 'Heh, heh, heh, / Who knows what evil lurks in the hearts of men? The Shadow knows.' / O, yes he does / O, yes he does. / An evil word it is, / This Love." [6] Is it possible that even in this early poem Jones underlines his doubt by such insistent repetition, as he does with the capitalization and triple punctuation of "THERE *MUST* BE A LONE RANGER!!!"? [7] Love is easily

---

[6] "In Memory of Radio," *Preface,* pp. 12–13.
[7] "Look for You Yesterday, Here You Come Today," *Preface,* p. 17.

reversed, naturally, and when it is it becomes evil—as Jones points out more than once. He seems aware, early on, in his frequently anthologized "The New Sheriff," that if there is no Lone Ranger, he may have to become himself a sheriff. As he says, what is in him is "so cruel, so / silent," that "it hesitates / to sit on the grass / with the young white / virgins." [8] The call to action is insistent, though "The New Sheriff" is more realistically considered a poem of hesitation, or perhaps preparation for action. But "Green Lantern's Solo" is more explicit. Green Lantern, one of the comic book heroes who is conspicuously less white than, say, Lamont Cranston or Superman, functions in the metropolis, working directly in the streets to cope with innumerable wrongs. Of all things, Green Lantern is an apotheosis of action.

What Jones seems to fear in "Green Lantern's Solo" is dying "without knowing life." He offers examples: "My friend, the lyric poet, / who has never had an orgasm. My friend, / the social critic, who has never known society, / or read the great italian liars, except his father." But for all his worry and all his concern, the poem ends not with a call to action, but with a series of questions and comments which challenge man's ability to act by himself. "What man unremoved from his meat's source, can continue / to believe totally in himself?" Only the fully ignorant, like "our leaders," or the "completely devious / who are our lovers. / No man except a charlatan / could be called 'Teacher'." The truth and the lie are so similar as to be indistinguishable; and the poem ends with an ambiguous and unsettling comment about the fact that men demand knowledge of One greater than themselves ("Who cannot but yearn / for the One Mind, or Right, or call it some God . . ."). Implying virtually that no man is an island, he says, "the islands of mankind have grown huge to include all life." Individual action is either anachronistic or impossible. Thus, Green Lantern in this poem is either solo or soloing. If he is solo, alone, it is only because he is fictional and removed "from his meat's source"; if he is soloing he is simply claiming the dependence he perceives in others.

The call to action is a call to violence in *Black Magic*. The machine gunners are called forward in "A Poem Some People Will Have to Understand" (p. 6), after the simple statement: "I am no longer a credit / to my race." In "The People Burning," he talks

---

[8] *Preface*, p. 42.

about alternatives: about the fact that his friends (or someone) want him to be other than black: "Now they ask me to be a jew or italian, and turn from the moment / disappearing into the shaking clock of treasonable safety, like reruns / of films, with sacred coon stars. To retreat, and replay; throw my mind out, / sit down and brood about the anachronistic God, they will tell you / is real" (p. 11). As he says, "it is a choice, now, and / the weight is specific and personal." He is prepared to make the choice, even if it is a choice which will wear him down: "The lone saver is knowing exactly / how far to trust what is real. I am tired already / of being so hopelessly right," he says in "Letter to Elijah Muhammad" (p. 12). In this first volume, *Sabotage*, of *Black Magic*, Jones' themes become steadily more involved in history and blackness. God is anachronistic if it is the Italian or Jewish God of his white friends. Even Eliot himself is repudiated openly in the final page of the volume: "Things / shovel themselves, from where they always are. Spinning, a / moment's indecision, past the vision of stealth and silence / Byron thought the night could be. Death blow Eliot Silence, dwindling away, in the 20th century" (p. 44). There are visions and revisions yet to come, while there is also the vision of stealth and silence, almost a Joycean cunning—along with an end to Eliot. A death blow.

*Target Study* begins, as it must, with an identification. Jones is concerned with the most central problem of all: who he is. He has revised his vision, chopped out Eliot and Eliot's God, and in a parody of the identity crisis (one of so many) in *A Portrait of The Artist as a Young Man* (when Stephen sees himself in terms of *"Europe / The World / The Universe"*) he says:

> I am real, and I can't say who
> I am. Ask me if I know, I'll say
> yes, I might say no. Still, ask.
>
> I'm Everett LeRoi Jones, 30 yrs old.
> A black nigger in the universe. A long breath singer,
> wouldbe dancer, strong from years of fantasy
> and study. ("Numbers, Letters," p. 47)

But there is a reality that Jones must deal with that is just as important as the reality of his own identity; it is the reality of the world and its ugliness. The early poems ("Confirmation," "Friday") mention its ugliness and describe it in almost the same surreal terms

Eliot uses in his "bats with baby faces" passage. The world is ugly, the white God is a "dingaling god" ("I Don't Love You") and "A white man / with / a dueling scar" ("Dada Zodji"). Jones recommends revolution ("Ration," p. 68) and rejoices that things are so serious for "White Eyes" that even "mailmen grow murderous offspring" ("Lowdown," p. 74). Yet, he can take a moment, as in "Western Front" (p. 81), to consider Ginsberg, who went to India to "see God," even if God is "sole dope manufacturer of the universe" and a "baldhead faggot."

"Western Front" has a poignancy that leads one to think Jones sympathizes deeply with Ginsberg's faith—though he cannot by any means share it. There is no India for Jones to travel to: "God / is not a nigger with a beard. Nor / is he not" (p. 90), and no amount of search, at this point in his quest, seems likely to bring him to the kind of peace he imagines for "fools" like Ginsberg. But the poignancy of "Western Front" is only a shadow of the poignancy of "Cold Term," a poem that seems clearly wishful and idealistic. If action is essential, and if action is violence, then Jones in his enthusiasm for the machine gunners is not blinded to what might have been and to what ought to be:

> Why cant we love each other and be beautiful?
> Why do the beautiful corner each other and spit
> poison? Why do the beautiful not hangout together
> and learn to do away with evil? Why are the beautiful
> not living together and feeling each other's trials?
> Why are the beautiful not walking with their arms around
> each other laughing softly at the soft laughter of black beauty?
> Why are the beautiful dreading each other, and hiding from
> each other? Why are the beautiful sick and divided
> like myself? (p. 91)

Such a lament is not novel and did not have to wait for LeRoi Jones for it to be expressed, but it is nonetheless poignant and moving. Jones has already admitted that men are islands operating independently ("Poem for Religious Fanatics," p. 89), and he sees that black men living in a white city will become sick and divided. But in "Cold Term," he admits that a beautiful thing has been lost, and that if the black man is sick and divided, he is too. The call to violence is by no means without its dues: and the black man has historically paid his dues. The something in him that is so cruel takes its toll, though not without his being aware of it.

The solution for reordering the future is not just to rid the land of whiteness. In "I Am Speaking of Future Good-ness and Social Philosophy," Jones declares, "Man is essential / to my philosophy, / man." And he says that the white man is a man, even though he is also the beast of the age. Thus: "we must become Gods. / Gigantic black ones. / And scare them back into the dirt" (p. 99). Eventually, Jones sees black men as Gods in "The Test" (p. 188), but they are Gods in the Miltonic (not the Dantesque) sense: Gods dispossessed and in hell. "Like Gods we are in hell, fallen, pulling now / against the gravity of the evil one himself. / Black streak from sun power. We are Gods, Gods, flying in black space." The entire poem is important; it establishes the end of the Jewish God—seen here with four Italian "mobster cops" and with the "four dragons" of Revelation. White people are seen as driving black people against their natures, and there is no alternative but "the upward gaze" "pulling now / against the gravity of the evil one himself." The black Gods must displace the white God. In "The Black Man is Making New Gods" (p. 205), Jones reviles the old hanged man as one who, by mimicking the black man's suffering, may well have distracted him from his purposes. He says, "The Fag's Death / they give us on a cross. To Worship. Our dead selves / in disguise. They give us / to worship / a dead jew / and not ourselves." And then, "the empty jew / betrays us, as he does / hanging stupidly / from a cross, in an oven, the pantomime / of our torture."

What Jones is calling for is an inversion. The white God must go. White morality—symbolized for Jones by the Italian mobster and the Jewish merchant—must be turned around: "The magic words are: Up against the wall mother / fucker this is a stick up!" Such an expression, in the final poem in the collection, effectively establishes, even in its "impolite" language, the purposes of inversion which have been alluded to from the early poems onward. This last poem, "Black People!" talks about robbery, taking what is needed, dancing in the streets, turning things upside down: "We must make our own / World, man, our own world, and we can not do this unless the white man / is dead."

"Black People!" is a poem of finality; there are no alternatives, no ambiguities. The call is to magic, the black magic of the title:

the dance is magic dance; the acts magic acts; the words magic words. In all this there is no tinge of the white God, the white values: all is expunged. The cross, we have been told, is "a double dirty cross, to hang your civilization." [9] The naked man has long since been dispensed of in "Biography" (p. 124), in an image of cruelty which is impressive even in its economy: "hangs / hangs / granddaddy / granddaddy, they tore / his / neck." The kyrie eleison is said for the entire civilization, including all those blacks who wish to remain aboard as servants, in "Madness" (pp. 162–65). So it should come as no surprise that Jones' final poem is a call to arms, a call to turn everything upside down. The disappointing part is that it is not so much a vision of what has been promised as of what has been done: "Black People!" is no vision of black men freeing themselves, of finding the new black God; it is a vision of the rioting in Newark, with all the streets and all the stores of Newark laid out for looting. What is looted is not likely to be what is needed; this poem is, for all its exhortatory power, short of the vision of the new blackness, the new beauty. Yet Jones never denies this; his interest is in the black man doing what he should not be doing: the black man cannot be a credit to his race, since the very concept is a white concept, born of worshipping the white God, the hero as victim. Evil has been turned backwards, to live, though he hardly expects the white man to understand this.

Yet, for all the inversions, God has not been lost sight of, and Jones' identity is not abandoned. As he indicates in "Stirling Street September" (p. 177), "WE WORSHIP THE SUN, / We are strange in a way because we know / who we are. Black beings passing through / a tortured passage of flesh." He even echoes Eliot again —despite his having formally given him the death blow earlier—in: "The will to be in tune / the depth of god / the will of wills thunder and rain / silence throws light and decision / to be in / tune / with / God . . . to be alone with the God of creation the / holy nuance / is all beings. / Is the melody, and rhythm / of / the dancing / shit / itself" (pp. 182–83). In "Human to Spirit, Humanism to Animals," he says, "We are reaching / as God for God / as human / knowing / spirit" (p. 203). But Jones also knows that there is such a thing as backsliding, that "We are all spies for god," [10]

[9] "Madness," *Black Magic,* p. 162.
[10] "Are there blues singers in russia?" *Black Magic,* pp. 184–85.

by which he seems to mean spies for the Jewish God, since he talks about betrayal, "coparmies," and the "jewish dog." "We expect some real shit. We expect to love all the things / somebody runs down to us. We want things, and are locked here, to the earth, / by pussy chains, or money chains, or personal indulgence chains" (p. 185). Such a moral view is almost puritanical, yet it is logical that Jones at this point would turn his back on material values. "Black People!" by comparison with this poem seems an earlier, less informed composition if only because the poem gives credence to the possibility that what black people take from white stores could be of use to them. But the "personal indulgence chains" seems a clear declaration of independence from a corrupt morality, or from a morality that is not dedicated to freeing black consciousness. Jones' contempt for what can be stolen from white stores figures plainly in one of the last poems in *Black Magic*: "Those Things. These refrigerators, stoves, / automobiles, airships, let us return to the reality of the spirit, / to how our black ancestors predicted life should be, from the / mind and the heart, our souls like gigantic kites sweep across / the heavens, let us follow them, with our trembling love for the world" (p. 223).

Thus the prose tracts Jones has written in recent years, since the publication of *Black Magic*, have consistently urged a firm moral position for the black man, one which unites him with his Black brothers and one that turns its back on white corruption. The logic of this position was begun in the earliest poetry and developed through the struggles with Eliot's conception of God, and through the ultimate creation of an alternative to Eliot's moral view.

It may be said that one of Jones' solutions to the dilemma of what to do about Eliot's God, and what to do about the existential heroes of his comic book youth, is to supplant them both in his own person. Eliot's God is seen as bankrupt and dangerous in *Black Magic*. If he is not abandoned entirely, he is transformed and played against. The comic book heroes change after "Green Lantern's Solo." One of the last references is in "Madness" (p. 164), in which even the Lone Ranger is untrustworthy. He says, " 'i'm hurt, help me, no stay with me nigger, / die with me nigger . . . no one will remember / Hi Yo Silver . . . Away!!' " The last apparent reference to Superman is ironic: "We have a nigger in a cape and cloak. Flying above the shacks and whores" ("Election Day—2," p. 213), a reference apparently to the mayoral election in Newark. It may not be realistic to see Jones imagining himself as a kind of God, though he has seen black men as gods; but there is a curious passage near the end of *Black Magic* that suggests the temptation may be present:

> I cd walk
> if I want to
> I used to run
> I can sing a little
> bit but that still
> don't say I can heal
> or bring back
> the dead ("Bumi," p. 196)

Facing this is a poem, "From the Egyptian," which issues forth a doctrine of revenge which rings of Old Testament zeal, not to mention Old Testament language. It begins: "I will slaughter / the enemies / of my father / I will slay those / who have blinded / him." And it ends: "car bashed into house fat legs / upside down, and smashed bloody JESUS / whatill we do, lets geh-uh ohh ra-ze ra-ze / I will slaughter the enemies of my father / I will slay those who have blinded him" (pp. 197–98).

Perhaps it is merely a vatic pose Jones adopts in these poems, and he does not apotheosize himself at all. But there is a curiosity that lingers in the imagination regarding the name he has assumed since the publication of his poems, the Islamic name which appears in the "Explanation" to *Black Magic*. One wonders if God and the comic book heroes are dead forever, or if they have been absorbed into Jones' poetic unconscious waiting to poke out again. His name, Báraka, like Lorca's Duende, means many things. Its root is Hebrew: Brk, and it means a number of things: lightning, the blessed of God, virtue, inspiration, the muse. "Since lightning is a phenomenon everywhere attributed to the gods, *báraka* means the sudden divine rapture that overcomes either a prophet or a group of fervent devotees." [11] It makes one think of the lightning bolt on Captain Marvel's chest, the faith that transformed a Billy Batson at the altar of Shazam, and the consequent faith that out of the scourge of action will come a new order, a new wholeness.

[11] Robert Graves, "The Word 'Báraka'," in *Oxford Addresses On Poetry* (New York: Doubleday & Company, Inc., 1962), p. 110.

# Baraka as Poet

*by Clyde Taylor*

The mark of LeRoi Jones' poetry is the mark of his personality
on the printed page. He is the most personal so far of the Afro-
American poets. For him poetry is the flow of being, the process of
human electricity interacting with the weight of time, tapped and
possibly trapped on paper. Feelings, impressions, moods, passions
move unedited through a structure of shifting images. Quick poems,
light on their feet, like a fancy middle-weight. Mostly, his poems
carry no argument, no extractable, paraphraseable statement. They
operate prior to the pros and cons of rational, persuasive, politic
discourse. Even after several readings, one is likely to remember
mainly a flavor, a distinct attitude of spirit, an insistent, very personal voice.

His poetry is written out of a heavy anti-rationalist, anti-didactic
bias. Its obligation is to the intentions of its own feelings. Its posture
is in defiance of criticism. The critic is for him the sycophant and
would-be legislator of official (white) reality, an implacable enemy,
the best symbol of the spiritually dead pseudo-intellectuality of the
West. (Lula in *Dutchman* is a white *critic,* if you watch closely.)
Against the strictures and constipations of this official reality, his
poetry is an imposition upon the reader of the actuality, the majesty
even (hence, LeRoi) of his subjectivity. The personalism of his
earlier poetry, particularly, is a challenge to the ready-to-wear definitions of the sociologically defined "Negro writer" lying in wait for
him.

The arrogance of *Preface to A Twenty Volume Suicide Note* and
*The Dead Lecturer* is in this personalism and intimacy, not in any

pretensions of impeccability of character. The poetry alternately invites the reader to jam his face into his own shit or to love or condemn the poet. It is the work of a spiritual gambler who wants to think of himself as waging heavy stakes. A reflection of this spirituality is its absoluteness. All his poems give the notion of being end-of-the-line thoughts, where attempts to reach an understanding dance on the edge of ambiguity. They are the works of an apprentice guru, "stuntin' for disciples," he later decided.

A major source of this creative orientation came from the streets. The hipsterism that nourished his poetry has to be regarded respectfully since whatever its limitations hipsterism was the germ of several cultural and social revolutions still turning in the world today. Hipsterism was a counter-assertion to brand-name, white values and the conformism of middle America, a serio-comic celebration of energies and forms unaccounted for, a mysticism (with some odd resemblances to Zen and other spiritual disciplines) of rhythms and tempos inside of and beyond metronomic, bureaucratic time, reflective of the polyrhythmic time of black music (particularly be-bop) and of the fluid, open time-space sensation of a pot high. Hipsterism was a new, Afro-American ontology, a style of knowing the world and acknowledging in the parody of one's own posture the craziness of a materialistic, hyper-rationalist, racist, self-contradictory square world on the one hand and the absurdity of a universe that mocked human values in its variousness and arbitrariness on the other.

An important aspect of hipsterism that LeRoi absorbed, less familiar than, say, the relationship to black music, was its deep fascination with the ghost-spirits and fantasy-figures of pop culture, the radio, movies, the comic book.[1] The connections between the aware black mind and these fantasy dramas are extremely complex, but a few linkages need to be suggested here. There was, first, the conviction that the world of sharp-edged pop invention, with all its ridiculous exaggeration, was a more accurate profile of the square world than it could afford to admit ("the white man, WHO AT BEST IS VERY VERY CORNY DUDE"—*BMP*, p. 163). There was also a contempt for the falsification of American manhood in

[1] See the very thoughtful article by Lloyd Brown, "Comic-Strip Heroes, LeRoi Jones and the Myth of American Innocence," *Journal of Popular Culture*, III (Fall, 1969), 191–204.

its stoical cowboys and tough detectives and a preoccupation with
drawing the social-political-racial connotations of such characters
as Gunga Din, King Kong, Rochester, Aunt Jemima and of such
relationships as the Lone Ranger–Tonto hook-up.

> My silver bullets all gone
> My black mask trampled in the dust
>
> & Tonto way off in the hills
> moaning like Bessie Smith.
> *(Preface . . . , p. 18.)*

But there was also a kind of envy felt by the hipster toward the
pop world in the feeling that its craziness was of an inferior aesthetic
texture than his own and then in an unfulfillable identification with
its outcast loner-heroes, many of whom (like Lamont Cranston and
The Shadow, Bruce Wayne and Batman, etc.) lived secret, powerful
identities apart from their bland but urbane public images and
who had extraordinary energies and powers available to them, or
who, like the detectives and cowboys, lived intense, dangerous, un-
social lives redeemed by the gloom and glamor of their inevitable
defeats.

When LeRoi moved uptown from the East Village in 1965—possibly the most momentous getaway in Afro-American or American
letters—he left much behind, but took much of this aesthetic with
him. Moving uptown, his poetry remained underground. To borrow
a figure whose fascination Jones shares with Blake, his poetry passes
through a vortex—a point at which physical forces converge—such
as the center of a whirlpool. Graphically, this passage might be
represented like this:

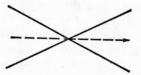

His development has been through one vortex into another (carrying
a large segment of creative Afro-America with him). A reading of
his works together shows that the crossing was not as sudden as its
results were profound. More important, at the convergence-point of

these two vortexes the themes, motifs, style, images are common to both, though sometimes inverted.

In brief, what we can see happening in *Black Magic Poetry, 1961–1967* is the despair without reference-point of the earlier volumes discovering its most sufficient cause in the enormity of the fall of man under whiteness. (See "Jitterbugs," *BMP*, 92.) Looking back, he admits, "I was under the spell of the whiteman," and *BMP* (and the plays, too) exhibits the violent and painstaking exorcism of the sick spirits that had possessed him. The fragments of a disjointed psyche crystallize themselves into new energies, heavier rhythms and shockingly concrete images:

> We want 'poems that kill.'
> Assassin poems, Poems that shoot
> guns. Poems that wrestle cops into alleys
> and take their weapons leaving them dead
> with tongues pulled out and sent to Ireland.
> *BMP*, 116.

The vagrant itches of his personal fantasies come home to a new cosmology, much indebted to Elijah Muhammad (see the dramatization of the Yacub myth in *Black Mass*). The natural order of the universe, in which "everything is everything" and man is in harmonious relation to nature and the gods, his imaginative and creative powers equal to his needs, has been interrupted disastrously by the intrusion of a counter-human homunculus (the white man) who maintains its parasitical existence feeding on the blood of living (nonwhite, essentially black) people and their cultures. A crucial image is the vampire: ". . . vampires, flying in our midst, at the / corner, selling us our few horrible minutes of discomfort and frus / tration." The homunculus and the spread of its civilization is the equivalent of the appearance of sickness, disease, maladjustment, and death into the universe, largely by virtue of its diabolical insinuation of abstraction (especially of time) and materialism, but also through enslavement of living cultures under the notion that it is God. The sensitive reader of E. Franklin Frazier's cool, objective *Race and Culture Contacts in the Modern World* can find in *Black Magic Poetry* an appropriate moral and imaginative rendering of a certain, credible view of history.

But to characterize Jones' poetry rather than a particular segment of black nationalist ideology is to recognize the residue of the earlier, personal world-view transformed in the uptown work. For instance, the particular, non-conformist "craziness" of the be-bopper, one indigenous reference point for the adolescent Leroy, becomes the "black madness" of "Black Dada Nihilismus" and then the holier black madness of the intense, fiery, disorienting (to whites) commitment to blackness of the third section of *BMP*. Or, the Baudelairean, *fin du monde* despair of the downtown poetry becomes, after the crossing, a despair of the dying West and a determination to slick its way toward its self-destruction. One other hang-over Baudelairean feature is the posture of the innocent damned, the pure spirit confounded by stultifying orthodoxy into a rebellion that consists of an inversion of orthodox values.

What emerges is a diabolism, incipient from the earliest poems, whose main feature is the blaspheming of the hated religion, in this case the religion of whiteness. It is a commitment implied in the title, *Black Mass,* or in the poem "Black Art" (for some oblique but real parallels see Cavendish's book, *The Black Arts,* a primer of the unholy and occult sciences) or in the whole conception of *Black Magic Poetry.* The black magic motive (*black* meant ironically) is the drive to weave an imaginative spell powerful and compelling enough to counteract in the minds of black people the spell of the white man for "To turn their evil backwards / is to / live," or (see the last page of *Home*):

> We are unfair, and unfair.
> We are black magicians, black art
> s we make in black labs of the heart.
>
> The fair are
> fair, and death
> ly white.
>
> The day will not save them
> and we own
> the night.

It is as though his talent were lying around like an empty bag until filled by the spirit-breath of suddenly conscious black people and took stunning shapes from the idioms, rhythms, folklore, the needs and crises, the beauties of a self-defining Afro-America. Some of the *Black Magic* poems adapt the forms of blacktalk: the dozens in "T. T. Jackson sings" and "Word from the Right Wing"; wall-writings like "You cannot hurt / Muhammud Ali, and stay / alive"; hoodoo curses like "Babylon Revisited" and "Sacred Chant for the Return of Black Spirit and Power," raps such as "Poem for Half-White College Students," put-downs like "CIVIL RIGHTS POEM" and neo-African chants such as "Part of the Doctrine" (p. 200). But more of the poems are free-form reflective lyrics, alternately public and private, in which Jones shows remarkable growth as "a long breath singer" in contrast to the telegraphese of the earlier work. In these, where the inspiration is street talk and the long, cascading line of Coltrane and what might be called the Eastern-Astral school of black music, the utterance moves in one unimpedable breath, with its own swoops, cries, distributed vocal parts, sound effects and faultlessly chosen words to its cymbal-crash ending. Poems like "Poem for Black Hearts" and "Black People" are among the few works equal to the intensity and urgency of the black rediscovery years of the sixties.

The incandescent furies of *BMP* subside in subsequent poems, some of them collected in *In Our Terribleness* (1970). It is as though Jones sensed that simple, diabolical inversion of white values is another form of flattery and dependency and that the creative motif of de-spelling the white man had run its course. The later poems, more independently reflective of the spiritual needs of black people, are mellower, less satiric, showing a deeper turn into mysticism. This latest change in a poet who believes in change as a fundamental aspect of reality is signaled by the adoption of a new name, Imamu Amiri Baraka.

There are enough brilliant poems of such variety in *Black Magic* and *In Our Terribleness* to establish the unique identity and claim for respect of several poets. But it is beside the point that Baraka is probably the finest poet, black or white, writing in this country these days. The question still has to be asked whether he has fulfilled the vocation set for him by his own moves and examples. He has called himself a "seer" (one familiar with evil is the way he defined it) and holy man, but hesitates to claim (while vying for it) the fate-ful name of prophet.

The prophet differs from the poet and other word-men in his role of awaking and sustaining among his people a vision of their destiny set beside the criteria of their deepest values in the most fundamental though significant language. A poet's obligation, by contrast, is to the integrity of his verbal rendering of his individual sensibility. The problem is whether Baraka's creative impulse, which is essentially underground, hip, urban, and avant-garde, can be made to speak for a nation of black people rather than for a set of black nationalists. Can he transcend the inclination to ad-lib on the changes of black consciousness (the way be-boppers ad-libbed on "Indiana") toward redefining that consciousness in the light of enduring values and in major works of sustained thought and imagination?

"We need a heavy book, like the Bible or the Koran," he writes in *In Our Terribleness*. This is doubtless too much to ask of one man. There are qualities, further, in his creative armament that run counter to that need. He seems to confuse fantasy, which is whimsical and gratuitous (consider "Answers in Progress" in *Tales*, 1967, and "All in the Streets" in *Terribleness*, both beautiful reveries) with myth, which, however non-rational its basis, holds firmly to a certain kind of cause-effect economy. His early avant-garde posture has given way to a mysticism that depends upon other people's orthodoxies, a gnosticism, really, that carries with it the aura of initiates, adepts and degrees of secret lore. The magic of his poetry owes almost as much to his enchantment with figures of pop culture like Mandrake, Lamont Cranston, Plastic Man, and The Green Lantern as it does to African cosmology and Arabic philosophers. Some of his symbols look like paraphernalia left over from a Shriner's convention. In his later work, black nationalism moves toward becoming a subdivision of the occult sciences, whereas something more broadbacked, comprehensive, open, accountable seems demanded by the ethos of black people—the kind of poetry (groping for a reference) Malcolm might have written, had he turned his genius in that direction.

The legacy of hipsterism, then, together with his still rather Baudelairean spiritual elegance, places Baraka's work always underground or aloft in relation to the meat and potatoes' scene where the straight world works out its dull, mediocre gimmicks. His peril is that his work must pass close to that fearful terrain—not conceding to whiteness all of the middle, ordinary world, where humans play out their messy lives—if it is going to take on the amplitude and range of black being.

The limitations I speak of, already dwindling in his latest pieces, really go beyond a consideration of Baraka as poet. *There*, the same qualities are adornments of his invented poetic cosmos, part of the spell-binding conviction of the work, adding tones to one of the distinctive, compelling, haunted modern voices, a voice like the nerve-endings of our terrible times. They are part of the legend, a legend supported by a list of accomplishments impressive in a writer just reaching midcareer. And he *has* become a prophet in the literary sense, establishing modes in which some of the most stirring impulses of black expressiveness have found form. Behind this record, still another title comes to mind for Baraka, one we used to confer only upon ourselves; he is "The Kid of Afro-American Writing."

# The Poetry of Three Revolutionists:
# Don L. Lee, Sonia Sanchez,
# and Nikki Giovanni

## by R. Roderick Palmer

W. E. B. Du Bois once said that "After the Egyptian and Indian, the Greek and Roman, the Teuton and Mongolian, the Negro is a sort of seventh son, born with a veil, and gifted with second-sight in this American world—a world which yields him no true self-consciousness, but only lets him see himself through the revelation of the other world. It is a peculiar sensation, this double-consciousness, this sense of always looking at one's self through the eyes of others, of measuring one's soul by the tape of a world that looks on in amused contempt and pity. One ever feels his two-ness—an American, a Negro; two souls, two thoughts, two unreconciled strivings; two warring ideals in one dark body, whose dogged strength alone keeps it from being torn asunder." [1]

Literature written by blacks in this country and elsewhere has had to include these forces to make them a reality, for they are forces that ferment revolution and nation-building. Writers of such literature are called revolutionists. Nick Aaron Ford, in his *Black Insights,* defined such writers as those who "have expressed allegiance to the revolutionary movement dedicated to the rejection of current American standards of morality, justice, education, social behavior, beauty, and aesthetics and their replacement by black standards

[1] W. E. B. Du Bois, *The Souls of Black Folk* (Chicago: A. C. McClurg and Company, 1903), p. 3.

tailored to fit the exclusive feelings and needs of the black American subculture." [2]

Literature by blacks which does not seek to achieve these standards is irrelevant to black people in these times. Although these standards fuse, they also have separate characteristics. Revolution must give definition to the nation. Revolution must call for and act to bring about an end to white supremacy, colonialism, and oppression embodied in Western ideas which affect and infect the existence of black people. The process of nationhood must conceptualize and structure the projections and possibilities of black existence.

The poetry of three very pronounced revolutionary black writers, Don L. Lee, Sonia Sanchez, and Nikki Giovanni, does just that. Readers find in their war cries no conclusions or inferences which fail to follow premises or evidence upon which they are based. Their exhortations contain no appeal to a reader's prejudice, self-interest, and superiority complex without reason. Thus, no *ad hominem,* no *non sequitur* in their writing! Their poetry promulgates the black aesthetic, revitalizes black values, and delineates the natural spirit of black people to the end that security, respect, and equality shall be the foundations of black life.

As revolutionary black poets, Lee, Sanchez, and Giovanni write what is labeled protest literature, a term often bestowed upon any work by black writers. John Howard Griffin declares they cannot help but "scream, yell, and shout." Thus, many critics say protest poetry is inferior.

Addison Gayle, in the preface to his *Black Expression,* declares that "the most important reason for the inferior status of Negro literature stems from the social mores deeply embedded in the American psyche. A nation incapable of recognizing Negroes as other than inferior beings—hewers of wood and drawers of water—has been unable to transcend the myths used to buttress the arguments of slaveholders and modern-day segregationists." [3]

He goes on to say that "Such concepts have led to certain corollaries: Negroes are unlikely to produce important literature, or to undergo the kinds of experiences, universal in character, which form the basis of competent literature. For if one views the Negro through

[2] Nick Aaron Ford, *Black Insights* (Waltham, Massachusetts: Ginn and Company, 1971), p. 303.

[3] Addison Gayle, Jr., ed., *Black Expression* (New York: Weybright and Talley, 1969), p. viii.

the sociological microscope, his inferiority mandates that his progeny too will be inferior. The old myths, therefore, remain. Black is inferior, of a poorer quality than white; black people as a result are different beings, existing in narrow worlds, enclosed by petty experiences—experiences unrelated to the national character." [4] Viewed in the light of these deeply ingrained concepts, Gayle further points out that some critics feel that "Negro literature is simplistic, immature, and unimportant." [5] The point of this essay is to disprove this shibboleth, for the Negro writer has been concerned with crucial problems of life, in a physical and moral sense, in a society in which Negro life has been the most expendable commodity. Hence, literature, dealing with such serious subject matter, cannot, in essence, be simplistic, immature, and unimportant. Thus let us consider first the poetry of Don L. Lee and note his treatments of the myriad of subject matter.

In Lee's essay "Black Poetics / for the many to come," found in his volume of poems, *Don't Cry, Scream,* he says "that most, if not all, blackpoetry will be *political.* I've often come across black artists . . . who feel that they and their work should be apolitical; not realizing that to be apolitical is *to be* political in a negative way for blackfolks. There is *no* neutral blackart; either it *is* or it *isn't,* period. . . . Blackpoetry will continue to define what *is* and what *isn't.* Will tell what is *to be* & how to *be* it (or bes it). Blackpoetry *is* and will continue to be an important factor in culture building." [6]

One of the most current and vital protests on the American scene today is women's liberation. Lee is well-known for his poetic accolades to the black woman. He feels that the black woman could use a strong black male image to arrive at herself—

> blackwoman:
> is an
> in and out
> rightsideup
> action-image
> of her man. . . . . . .
> in other
> (blacker) words;
> she's together,

[4] *Ibid.,* p. ix.
[5] *Ibid.*
[6] Don L. Lee, *Don't Cry, Scream* (Detroit: Broadside Press, 1969), p. 16.

> if
> he
> bes.[7]

Lee writes about the assassination of Martin Luther King and Malcolm X. About King he says:

> it was wild.
> the
> bullet hit high.
>                     (the throat-neck)
> & from everywhere:
>     the motel, from under bushes and cars,
>     from around corners and across streets,
>     out of the garbage cans and from rat holes
>     in the earth
> they came running.
> with
> guns
> drawn
> they came running
> toward the King—
>                     all of them
>                     fast and sure—
> as if
> the king
> was going to fire back.
> they came running,
> fast and sure,
> in the
> wrong
> direction.

Lee's long poem for Malcolm X is entitled "Malcolm Spoke / who Listened? (this poem is for my consciousness too)," and further says of him, "he speaks of the prostitution of blackness, that is, denial of the self-asserted black."

In "a poem for negro intellectuals (if there bes such a thing)," Lee refers to

> a people deathliving
> in

⁷ Don L. Lee, *Don't Cry, Scream*, p. 55. All other poems referred to in this section of the essay were taken from this volume.

> abstract realities
> hoping / looking
> for
> blk / man-actions
> from
> action-livers.

While, in his "History of The Poet as a Whore," dedicated "(to all negro poets who deal in whi-te paronomasia)," he writes

> yeats in brown-tone
> ultrablack with a whi-te tan,
> had a dangerous notion that
> he / she
> wd be famous yesterday.
> a paper prostitute
> with ink stained contraceptions.
> still,
> acute fear of colored pregnancy
> forces poet to be poet
> & not "negro poet" (supposedly a synonym for blk /poet)
> whose poem-poems are conceived in
> nine month intervals
> with a
> rarity of miscarriages tho most are
> premature.

Lee strongly believes that education in white America teaches the black man *how not to be Black*. In a typical poem, from his volume *Think Black*—a poem, entitled "Wake-up Niggers"—he says, parenthetically, "(you ain't part Indian)." And in "Back Again Home," also found in *Think Black,* he tells us that to rediscover his blackness, the black man has to resign from white values. Once he does this, Lee says, he is "Back Again, BLACK AGAIN, Home."

Although the black man's blackness is often the topic for serious treatment, Lee is capable of seeing humor in it, too, at times. In his poem "But He Was Cool or: he even stopped for green lights," he writes of the "cool cat" who is so anxious to be black that he is "super-cool ultrablack." He wears a double-natural "that wd put the sisters to shame"; is, in fact, "cool-cool so cool him nick-named refrigerator."

What is Don L. Lee's hangup? The answer seems to be concerned with his impatience with "niggers" and "negroes" (he uses the terms synonymously) who refuse to be Black, and with "little niggers killing little niggers" as he tells us in his poem "Nigerian Unity"—

> little niggers
> killing
> little niggers.
> the weak against the weak.
> the ugly against the ugly.
> the powerless against the powerless.
> the realpeople becoming unpeople
> & brothers we have more in common
> than pigmentation & stupidity.

In "a poem to complement other poems," the poet places emphasis on *change:*

> change.
> life if u were a match i wd light u into something
>     beautiful. change.
> change.
> for the better into a realreal together thing.
>     change, from a make believe
> nothing on corn meal and water, change.
> . . . know the realenemy, the world's enemy.
>     know them know them know them the
> realenemy change your enemy change your change
>     change change your enemy change change
> change change your change change change.
> your
> mind nigger.

Lee's last poem in the volume is full of confident hope and optimism for black people and what they will eventually accomplish. He calls it "A Message All Blackpeople Can Dig (& a few negroes too)."

> we are going to do it.
> US: blackpeople, beautiful people; the sons and
>     daughters of beautiful people.
> bring it back to
> US: the unimpossibility.
> now is
> the time, the test

> while there is something to save (other than our lives).
> we'll move together . . .
> discover new stars: . . .
> blackpeople
> are moving, moving to return
>   this earth into the hands of
> human beings.

Sonia Sanchez, like Don L. Lee, is concerned with black identity. Within this framework, however, she manages to achieve an amazingly wide variety of treatments. Like Lee, she feels that the return to black identity is a "home-coming" (the title, by the way, of her first published volume of verse) after a sojourn in a white-oriented society geared to UN-black the Black man—to mold him to a white standard of values. She says in the poem "Homecoming"—

> i have been a
> way so long
> once so long
> i returned tourist
> style to watch all
> the niggers kill
> themselves . . .
>
> i have returned
> leaving behind me
> and those hide and
> seek faces peeling
> with freudian dreams
> this is for real.
>
>                       black
>           niggers
>                       my beauty[8]

In another poem, "to blk / record / buyer," she cautions blacks not to be deluded by the "blue-eyed soul brother."

> don't play me no
> righteous bros.
>
>                 white people
> aint rt bout nothing
> no mo.

[8] Sonia Sanchez, *Homecoming* (Detroit: Broadside Press, 1969), p. 9. All other poems referred to in this section of the essay are from this volume.

Again, like Lee, she is concerned with black manhood and, in her poem "to all brothers," sternly warns the black man not "to shack up with white chicks." And in a companion poem, "to all sisters," she asks

> What a white woman got
> cept money trying to buy up
> a blk / man?
> yeah.

It is Sonia Sanchez's belief that the orientation to blackness should start early. School children need redefinitions. They have been brainwashed to stereotypes by white teachers. What is a policeman? she asked one little black girl. The child's answer was typical: "He is a man who protects you." This is not the answer the poet gives. In her poem "in definition for blk / children," she says that to the ghetto child, a policeman is

> a pig
> and he shd be in
> a zoo . . .
> and
> until he stops
> killing blk / people
> cracking open their heads
> remember
> the policeman
> is a pig

To her eighth grade class in New York City—with children, many of whom had never before been taught by a black person—she says in "poem for dsc 8th graders—1966–1967":

> look at me 8th
> grade
> i am black
> beautiful. i have a
> man who looks at
> my face and smiles.

Sonia Sanchez can be tender and warm as these words from her "personal letter no 2" attest:

> if i were young
> i wd stretch you
> with my wild words.

She can be mystical and introspective as exemplified in her "poem at thirty":

> It is midnight
> no magical bewitching
> hour for me . . .
>
> father do not
> send me out
> among strangers.

As her mood changes, some of her poems display a peculiar humor; others reveal a disdainful spirit; and still others show that she can be mean and angry, at times. In her poem "for unborn malcolms," she is indignant and belligerent:

> git the word out
> now.
>     to the man / boy
> taking a holiday
> from murder.
>     tell him . . .
> the next time he kills one
> of our
>     blk / princes
>         some of his faggots
> gonna die
>     a stone / cold / death.
>                 yeah.
> it's time
>     an eye for an eye
>     a tooth for a tooth . . .
>         git the word
> out that us blk / niggers
>         are out to lunch.
> and the main course
> is gonna be his white meat.
>                 yeah.

As a protest poet, like Don L. Lee, Sonia Sanchez chooses themes from a wide range of the so-called "black experience." Her poems,

however, are more personalized. She uses the first person "i" more
frequently, and equates the black experience within the realm of
her own identity as a black woman. Nevertheless, she is never
maudlin. "A poet must never succumb to self-pity," she says. Self-
pity spells the death of poetry. Her poems are strong, direct, and
forcefully articulate in the free verse idiom of contemporary verse.

Of the three poets chosen for discussion, Nikki Giovanni is perhaps the most polemic, the most incendiary; the poet most impatient
for change, who thus advocates open violence as stated in the
poem "The True Import of Present Dialogue Black vs. Negro":

> Nigger
> Can you kill
> Can you kill
> Can a nigger kill
> Can a nigger kill a honkie
> Can a nigger kill the Man
> Can you kill nigger
> Huh? nigger can you
> kill
> Do you know how to draw blood
> Can you poison . . .
> A nigger can die
> We ain't got to prove we can die
> We got to prove we can kill . . .
> Learn to kill niggers
> Learn to be Black men[9]

Again, she says in her "Poem for Black Boys"

> Ask your mother for a Rap Brown gun
> Santa just may comply if you wish hard enough . . .
> DO NOT SIT IN DO NOT FOLLOW KING
>             GO DIRECTLY TO STREETS
>         This is a game you can win . . .
>
>     And you will understand all too soon
> That you, my children of battle, are your heroes
> You must invent your own games and teach us old ones
>     how to play[10]

[9] Nikki Giovanni, *Black Feeling, Black Talk* (Detroit: Broadside Press, 1970),
pp. 11–12.
[10] Nikki Giovanni, *Black Judgement* (Detroit: Distributed by Broadside Press,
1968), p. 5. All other poems referred to in this section of the essay are from this
volume.

In "A Litany for Peppe," she says

> Blessed is he who kills
> For he shall control this earth

"I wanted to write a poem that rhymes with revolution," she tells us in her lines penned "For Saundra" . . .

> but revolution doesn't lend
> itself to be-bopping
>
> then my neighbor
> who thinks i hate
> asked—do you ever write
> tree poems—i like trees
> so i thought
> i'll write a beautiful green tree poem
> peeked from my window
> to check the image
> noticed the school yard was covered
> with asphalt
> no green—no trees grow
> in manhattan
>
> then, well, i thought the sky
> i'll do a big blue sky poem
> but all the clouds have winged
> low since no-Dick was elected
>
> so i thought again
> and it occurred to me
> maybe i shouldn't write
> at all
> but clean my gun
> and check my kerosene supply
>
> perhaps these are not poetic
> times
> at all

Although Nikki Giovanni occasionally lends herself to less explosive themes in her two books *Black Judgement* and *Black Feeling, Black Talk,* essentially her main concerns display the open, revolutionary temperament of the aggressive activist. She has little patience with slow change, and exhorts Black Americans to rise up and take arms, for "Blessed be machine guns in Black hands." [11]

[11] See the poem "A Litany for Peppe."

Thus, in the poetry of these three revolutionists, we see corrosive satire and stark realism made all the more striking in that its outrage is presented in a uniquely abbreviated, yet comprehensive language. The writers speak in the voices of thoughtful revolutionaries, and employ appropriate informal contemporary idioms. Their rhetorical problem lies in making us forget the horrors blacks have suffered in this country and elsewhere, and in making us hearken to the clarion call for self-actualization, change, and revolution. The style and rhythm and the vocabulary and syntax are all based upon traditions set by past revolutionary writers, but updated and individualized by each poet to suit modern times. The use of the four-letter word and other obscenities, the abbreviated word, the slashed word, the fused word, the small letter "i," and the omission of capital letters and certain punctuation marks are—in themselves—experimentally revolutionary, and befit the poetic utterances of revolutionary writers. Thus, in this light, no fault can be found with their extravagant exercise of poetic license. Regarding their subject matter, common points of view, growing out of the Black Experience, are represented, and the poets do not straddle issues or mince words in discussing their themes. Problems of selection have been intensified and complicated by other more substantive problems. Their writers have battled the unique handicaps posed by the peculiar history of racial attitudes and actions in their native land, and they have battled well. In the 1960's in this country, a change occurred in the attitudes of the masses of both blacks and whites, and a search for a common identity was begun. Thus, the path depicted by the poetry of Lee, Sanchez, and Giovanni—depending upon circumstances and future developments—could lead in either of two directions, the direction of revolution or evolution.

# The New Poetry of Black Hate

## by *Arthur P. Davis*

Since the late 1950's, a new type of Negro American poetry has come into being, a poetry whose subject matter is unlike that of any other poetry heretofore produced by Negroes. It is a poetry based on and motivated by "poetic" hatred for white Americans and for everything associated with them, including middle class Negroes. It is only fair to say that not all recent poetry by Negro writers deals in hate, but a surprising amount of it does. I am concerned here with a sampling of this new literature and its critical concepts.

Angry poetry is not new for the Negro author. Almost from the very beginning, he wrote verses which protested America's treatment of her black citizens. Even a poet actually in slavery like George Moses Horton felt called upon to protest gently his lot: "Alas! and am I born for this / To wear this slavish chain?" And equally as unexpected, a professional accommodationist like Paul Laurence Dunbar produced a few mild protest poems. In fact, most Negro poetry prior to the late 1950's may be called protest writing; and yet, before this present era no Negro author of consequence wrote *hate* poems. There are poems bitterly attacking American hypocrisy and injustice; there are poems dealing with heroic self-defensive violence, but few if any poems of hate and no poems advocating hate as a policy.

The nearest *approach* (and I emphasize the word)—the nearest approach to earlier hate poetry came in the first decades of this century in the verses of W. E. B. Du Bois and Claude McKay. One of the bitterest poems of the period is "A Litany at Atlanta," written by Du Bois after the 1906 riot in that city. [In this poem] one . . . notes that for Du Bois the hatred is to be God's hatred of evil-doing

"The New Poetry of Black Hate," by Arthur P. Davis. From *CLA Journal,* XIII no. 4 (June 1970), 382–91. Copyright © 1970 by the College Language Association. Reprinted by permission of the author and the publisher.

and the vengeance God's punishment, not the hatred and vengeance of the victimized Negroes. And in spite of the horrible thing that has happened, the poet expresses faith in God's existence and in God's ultimate justice. . . . still the God of our black fathers . . ." In brief, though he was not a conventional Christian, Du Bois speaks, as did practically all of the Negro poets of that generation, from the climate of an accepted Christian faith, a climate in which hate had no place.

Claude McKay could also write with a searing bitterness, and because of his color and his caste-ridden West Indian childhood, he probably held a deeper animosity towards American whites and their civilization than Du Bois. But McKay made of his feelings a hardening, shaping force. I will go, he says in effect, into your "hottest zone" of hatred, and I will come out, not bitter and frustrated, but a "stronger soul." This is the theme of "Baptism." In "White Houses," he tells us that: ". . . I must keep my heart inviolate / Against the potent poison of your hate." Note again that it is "your hate," that is, white rather than black hatred; and the persona, though "sharp as steel with discontent," is determined to rise above the level of revenge and eye-for-an-eye retaliation.

One could cite literally hundreds of similar protest poems from writers like Langston Hughes, Countee Cullen, Sterling A. Brown, Melvin B. Tolson, Gwendolyn Brooks, and others—poems which, whatever their themes, never expressed or implied hate as a weapon in the Negro's arsenal. Such a stand would have been not only alien to the Christian background from which the authors sprang (and I am not speaking of their personal beliefs), but would have also seemed to them an unworthy stooping to the level of the enemy. As a matter of record, a few of the early New Negro poets tended to be a little smug about their superior patience and charity. "Brother, come!" / writes Joseph Seamon Cotter, Jr., "And let us go unto our God. / And when we stand before Him / I shall say— / 'Lord, I do not hate, / I am hated . . . / And, brother, what shall you say?' "

How different is the climate today! Charles Anderson's "Prayer to the White Man's God" is typical of the new attitude: "I been prayin' for centuries / To some God up in the sky. / . . . God said, *Go 'way boy* / *I don't want to hear you cry*, / But I know Jesus heard me / Cause he spit right in my eye." This sneering contempt for Christianity is, of course, not limited to Black militant writers, but it serves as a spawning ground for the new doctrine of hatred found in their poetry.

Ironically enough, the reasons for hating whitey were far stronger in the days of this generation's fathers and grandfathers than they are now. Though by no means full-fledged citizens, Negroes at the present time have more freedom, more political, educational, and industrial opportunities, more of everything that the American way of life offers than at any other time in the Negro's history. But not a single new poet that I have read ever mentions this fact. According to the rules for running a revolution, Black or otherwise, any such concession to facts would be the rankest kind of treason. It would also show weakness. The supporters of a revolution must insist that the present order is *all* wrong, and regardless of truth or reason or any other consideration must support this stand to the bitter end. And that is what the Black revolutionists and the recent Black poets have done with regard to whitey and his Establishment.

It hasn't been hard for the leaders of this Black Revolution to build up hatred for whitey in the youngsters of today. They have inherited the frustrations, humiliations, and resentments of countless generations who were unable to express their feelings because of many fears and pressures. But this generation fears nothing, has no shibboleths. It is free in a sense that no other Negro generation has been, and it has made the most of this freedom by unloosing an avalanche of hatred on all of the old lies, the old hypocrisies, and the old shams their fathers had to endure. Moreover, the times are with them in another way. They are part of a world movement. Young people everywhere are tired of the old order and are rebelling against it. Black revolutionists obviously have far more reason to destroy the old order of things than the white, and they have therefore been more strident and more insistent in their demands for a new world. In the swift logic of revolutionary thinking, whitey has become the symbol of all that is to be exterminated. Naturally, he has become the prime theme of the new Black poetry, the one from which lesser themes take root.

The high priest of this new Black literary renaissance and the one who has done most to shape its course is the talented, many-

sided LeRoi Jones. In "Black Arts," Jones keynotes the movement:
"We want 'poems that kill,' " he writes, "Assassin poems, poems that
shoot / guns. . . . / We want a black poem. And a Black World."
The two-fold idea of destroying and rebuilding runs through most
of this hate poetry. Through "art" as an instrument and a weapon,
we "kill" the old and build a new Black Jerusalem.

In "Transcendental Blues," Yusuf Rahman points out that it
is the black man's mission and destiny to rain "drops-of-hate" on
"them," erasing and exterminating them, "so humanity can have a
clear slate. . . ." If "them" means all of the whites, the new humanity, I take it, will consist of the colored peoples of the world.
Or does he have in mind only American whites?

The attitude of Lance Jeffers is ambivalent and a little broader.
In his poem, "My Blackness is the Beauty of this Land," he declares
"my love and yet my hate shall civilize this land," shall be "this
land's salvation." In another poem he asks for "rugged hate" and
"sturdy oaktree love" to make a new nation with a black soul "and
America shall cease to be its name."

The concept of the Negro's mission to build a new and better
world is common to all of these poets. "Tomorrow is ours" is a
constantly repeated theme. In many poems and in some criticism,
the writers state with confidence that the world's future is Black,
and *Black* as used here means a philosophy, a morality, and a
religion based on the experiences and the sufferings of Africans and
Afro-Americans.

Lance Jeffers uses the love-hate theme seriously, I believe; but
Kuwasi Balagon has tongue-in-cheek when he writes the following
title: "If You Love Them, Wouldn't / You Like to See Them
Better Off?" The poet then asks: "What do you see in a tired ole
water-logged cracker's face." You must, he advises, "kill him for
his own good, roll his head with love / If you cannot hate." Note
the implication: if you can't fulfill your obvious duty, which is to
hate, then fall back on love, a lesser accomplishment. The poet
here speaks of whitey (and symbolically of Western civilization)
as he would of an old dying animal that should be put out of its
misery.

Many of these hate poems use whitey's alleged physical impotence
as a symbol of the decay of the Western tradition. In "Elements of

Grammar," Calvin C. Hernton scornfully comments on whitey's "little wee wee tucked under / The folds of his flabby belly" and calls him "the cock roach of civilization." (Perhaps the most vitriolic contempt for the white man's supposed physical and sexual impotence is found not in the poetry but in LeRoi Jones's drama, *The Slave*.)

Giving this contempt a new slant, DT OGILVIE, in his "Last Letter to the Western Civilization," agrees ironically with Balagon that one should have pity for the disabled: ". . . you mothering hypocrite / i feel sorry for you / as i would a cripple or a blind man / i pity you / for you are crippled of human-ness / human essence / human emotion. . . ." Because of guilt, the poet continues, Western civilization will see the Black handwriting on the wall and do away with itself. One cannot miss the supreme contempt implied in this thought.

Oftentimes the poets use a fire image when they write of extermination, and it is highly appropriate for their beliefs. Fire cleanses and purifies as it destroys. Destruction by fire is prophesied in the lines from a Negro spiritual: "No more water but the fire next time." And fire suggests the kind of phoenix-like death and resurrection these poets emphasize. In his fire poem, "Arson and Cold Lace (or how i yearn to Burn Baby Burn)," Worth Long is abusively frank: "We have found you out / False Faced America . . . / For now is the fire / and fire won't answer / To logic and listening . . . / Hot flames must devour. . . ." For S. E. Anderson in "A New Dance," ". . . Black is the spiralfire through corridors / of white halls enflaming / The white one must be cremated to be saved / and we must cremate to be saved / . . . and we dance the Black-flame dance / in tune to the rhythm of our times / . . . cleansing-fire spreads from city to city / to country to country / to world." "The Song of Fire" by Rolland Snellings is even more violent and specific: "Bright red flames. Burnt, charred death, / . . . will vindicate the blues; sanctify the earth / resurrect the mangled Jesus from . . . the Nordic lynch-tree! / (Fire) / will cauterize the Racist Plague!"

The extermination of whitey and his civilization by fire or otherwise is not advocated by these poets just to build a better world; it also satisfies a deep-rooted (that is, in poetry) desire for revenge. In

"Black Warrior," Norman Jordan falls back on atavistic urgings: "At night while / whitey sleeps / the heat of a / thousand African fires / burns across my chest . . . / Enchanted by this / wild call / I hurl a brick through / a store front window / and disappear." To see the difference between the climate of the New Negro Renaissance and that of the present time, compare this poem with Cullen's "Heritage," which has a similar atavistic background.

Jordan's window-smashing revenge is mild when placed beside that of Harry Edwards in "How to Change the U.S.A." Edwards suggests that "For openers, the Federal Government, the honkies, the pigs in blue" must all go down South, catch the men who blew up those four Negro girls, and "chop them up with dull axes. / Slowly. . . ." They must do this "Just as a gesture / of good faith." Again, to see the contrast between the two climates mentioned above, compare Langston Hughes' poem on the same incident, "Birmingham Sunday (September 15, 1963)," the last lines of which are: "Four little girls / Might be awakened some day soon / By songs upon the breeze / As yet unfelt among magnolia trees."

In Lefty Sims, the revenge motif takes on a religious coloring. In "An Angel's Prayer," he pleads: "Send me O'Allah as a / Rampaging fire, to consume, your / Enemy, as I praise your name." With "dear Allah's" backing, he wants to become "a sword of vengeance / to repay this Crafty Devil, . . ." He wants to adorn his neck "with the skulls of devils. . . ." The Black Muslims' concept of the creation of the white man by the evil Yacub gives religious sanction to the hate-and-revenge theme.

These new Black Arts writers hate middle class Negroes almost as much as they detest whites, and they divide all Americans into three groups: *whitey* or *honkeys; "Negroes";* and *Blacks* (not a minority but God's chosen few). A "Negro" in this division is a middle class Afro-American who still tries to be and act like the best white folks, who still feels that *integration* rather than *separatism* is the goal of our fight for freedom in America. A "Negro" (often in quotes) is also known as an Uncle Tom, as a nigga (note the spelling), as a brief-case nigger, and as an Oreo-nigger (like the cookie, black on the outside but disgustingly white inside). All "Negroes," of course, are traitors to the Black cause.

In "My Brother," James Danner scathingly denounces this traitor: ". . . Look at yourself, / With your little moustache and greased hair / And looking more like a Spaniard every day, / You fear the nigger in you. . . . / You are a nigger's nigger: / A white man in the head."

For these poets of hate, the lowest form of treason is for a "Negro" to become a pig. Bobb Hamilton's "Poem to a Nigger Cop" refers to this kind of defector as a "Black skin in a blue mask," also as "a big black no nuts nigger," who would be capable of shooting his own mother to uphold the white man's law if he caught her looting. The poem not too subtly implies that looting is somehow routine for ghetto dwellers.

The contempt of Welton Smith in "The Nigga Section" is even more withering: ". . . you have torn out your own tongue / you have made your women / to grow huge dicks . . . / you are the dumbest thing / on the earth the slimiest most rotten thing in the universe. . . ." In another poem with the involved title: "Special Section for the Niggas on the Lower Eastside or: Invert the Divisor and Multiply," Smith scathingly accuses these "niggas" of being "deranged imitators / of white boys acting out a / fucked notion of the mystique / of black suffering . . . / you are frauds . . . / you are jive revolutionaries / who will never tear this house down. . . ." These poets, one notes, are much harder on pseudoblacks (that is, Negroes who talk the Revolution but whose hearts still aren't with it)—much harder on these "jive revolutionaries"—than they are on Uncle Toms.

There are hundreds of poems written in this hate vein, but the ones given, I believe, are sufficient to illustrate the type. Before summarizing, however, I would like to say a word about the Black Arts criticism which has come into existence along with the new poetry. The prime mover and chief architect of this movement, as noted above, is LeRoi Jones, and Larry Neal is his articulate Prophet. Writing in the Black Theatre issue of *tdr* (Summer, 1968), Neal explains the new esthetics in an essay called "The Black Arts Movement." Using the works of Jones as a springboard, Neal tells us that the movement is "opposed to any concept of the artist that alienates him from his community"; that it is the "aesthetic and spiritual sister of the Black Power concept"; that "it proposes a separate symbolism, mythology, critique, and iconology"; and that it seeks a "cultural revolution in art and ideas." Neal is convinced that "the cultural values inherent in Western history must either be radicalized or destroyed," but he doubts that they can be radicalized. And then he adds several things that have now become expected: that Black artists must be accountable only to Black people; that Black art must not be "protest art" because that would defeat its primary aim; and that it must be ethical. The rest of this article by Neal deals specifically with Black Arts drama.

Though not as well known or as influential as Larry Neal, Clarence Major has been an able apologist for this new poetry. In the "Editor's Introduction" to his *The New Black Poetry,* Major has an eleven-page essay which states the aim of this new poetry in erudite and technical terms. It seems to me, however, that in his article in *Black Voices* entitled "A Black Criterion" is a clearer statement of his position. The Black poet, he insists, must isolate himself from Western culture and civilization, must "define himself," "must chop away at the white criterion and destroy its hold on his black mind" because to see the world through white eyes "causes death." Major believes that the Black poet is the "eye" of the West, and "We must use our black poetic energy to overthrow the Western ritual and passion, the curse, the dark ages of this death, the original sin's impact on a people and their unjust projection of it upon us black people; . . . With the poem, we must erect a spiritual black nation we can all be proud of." This, of course, sounds impressive, but how does one do it? Major is vague on that issue.

Another critic is James T. Stewart, whose article in *Black Fire* is entitled "The Development of the Black Revolutionary Artist." After a rambling disquisition on several things, some of them, it seems to me, not wholly pertinent, Stewart arrives at this conclusion: "The point of the whole thing is that we must emancipate our minds from Western values and standards. We must rid our minds of these values. Saying so will not be enough. We must try to shape the thinking of our people." He then tells us that the task of the Black writer "is revolutionary by definition" and that the Black writer "must view his role *vis-à-vis* white Western civilization, and from this starting point in his estrangement begin to make new definitions founded on his own culture—on definite black values."

Appearing in the *Negro Digest* (January, 1969), Carolyn F. Gerald in "The Black Writer and His Role" emphasizes "shaping an image for ourselves" to offset the "zero image" which has been projected upon the Black man by the white world and by Western culture. She believes that Black writers "are now proceeding with a vengeance" to smash the old idols; they are reversing the symbolism and using it as "the tool for projecting our own image upon the universe." She concludes her article with verses which, she believes, will illustrate her position by attempting "to desecrate the mythical and beautiful figure of the muse, entrenched in white culture" for so long. We note once more the destruction-rebirth fire imagery: "Dress the muse in black . . . / No! / Kill her! / Make her jump / Burning bright white bitch / From the pitched peak of our houses / Let her shriek / Pale old faded biddy . . . / Make it hot . . . / Clap and stomp the fire / And shout the spirit out of her. / And draw your circle close / For we'll kill us a devil tonight / . . . The fire's weak / And burned out / The universe is black again."

All of the critics presented here make the same major statements: there must be a new Black art, produced for Blacks from the destruction of the Western tradition. The trouble, however, is that no one yet has explained convincingly, at least to me, how Western artistic and cultural traditions are to be replaced. I also find in these poets no deeper awareness of what it means to be Black in a white world than I have found in Du Bois, McKay, Hughes, and more recently, Baldwin. In the meantime, the poets continue to put the new wine of their hatred into the old bottles of traditional forms. Although they use all kinds of gimmicks—peculiar spellings, lower case letters, abbreviations, unclosed quotation marks, fantastic line arrangements, intricate and lengthy titles, four letter words, African and Black Muslim names and images—in spite of these gimmicks, it is still Western poetry. The newness, except for the hate motivation, is about as meaningful as the change from a "kinked head" to a "bush."

And there are serious shortcomings: too much of this hate poetry is repetitive, mouthing over and over again the same revolutionary slogans and themes; some of it is guilty of bad taste, not moral but aesthetic, in using filth and obscenity only for the purpose of shocking the Establishment. And above all else, to a person of my age (over thirty) and background, an indiscriminate hatred of all whites seems too irrational to be tenable for long as motivation or inspiration. (Shades of John Ruskin!) But this raises another question: How *real* is the hate expressed in these poems? How much of this vitriolic verse is a pose or a convention? How much of it is a following of a "party line"? In my first paragraph I used the phrase *"poetic" hatred* because, after reading a considerable number of these poems, I get the same impression I receive from reading too many pastorals—the forms and conventions tend to stand out more clearly than anything else in the poems. During the Harlem Renaissance of the 1920's, most of the New Negro poets mouthed a kind of literary Garveyism (a superficial emphasis on African themes and images) that was never very convincing either to the poets themselves or to their readers. But McKay, Hughes, Cullen, and many others felt that they *had* to use the convention. Is the same thing happening today?

One final comment—there is a noteworthy difference between the new Black poetry and the new Black criticism. The hate element which is a staple of the poetry is not stressed as much in the critical works. This is a good sign; it augurs well for the future.

# Humanistic Protest in Recent Black Poetry

*by Richard K. Barksdale*

The tradition of protest against his social, political, and moral condition runs deep in the Black man's literature in America. It is not present in the poetry of Phillis Wheatley and Jupiter Hammon, but it is found in Olaudah Equiano's *Narrative of His Life* in 1789. It is found under the facetious poetic grin of George Moses Horton who, while drafting innocuous love songs for University of North Carolina undergraduates, could also bitterly complain:

> Alas! and am I born for this
> To wear this slavish chain?
> Deprived of all created bliss
> Through hardship, toil and pain!

It is found in the work of other antebellum Black poets like James Whitfield, Frances Watkins Harper, and Elymas Rogers. One even finds strains of social protest in some of the poetry and prose of that apostle of interracial good will, Paul Laurence Dunbar; for, underneath the sometimes mawkish sentimentality, there is the tight anger of "We Wear the Mask"—

> We sing, but oh the clay is vile
> Beneath our feet, and long the mile;
> But let the world dream otherwise,
> We wear the mask.

Certainly, protest is found throughout the innumerable cantos and versatile rhymes of Albery Whitman who, as a contemporary of Dunbar, produced a long poem of protest which is something of a Black literary first: *Rape of Florida* is the first protest poem of epic

"Humanistic Protest in Recent Black Poetry," by Richard K. Barksdale. This essay appears for the first time in this volume. Used by permission of the author.

length written in Spenserian stanzaic form about the twin tragedies
of the Indian and the Black man, using Longfellow's *Hiawatha* as
a literary model.

Elements of social and moral protest are also everywhere in the
Black man's folk literature—in his spirituals, his folk tales, his work
songs, his prison moans, his blues. One even finds some protest over
the Black man's social and economic condition in some of the heroic
bad man songs. In these the hero is usually so big and bad and
heroically self-sufficient that there is nothing in his path to protest about—like "Stackerlee" who "fought da debbil toe to toe /
Den blowed him down wid his forty-fo." But one does find strong
social protest in "Po Laz'us," a song about a young-ish bad man
who, with a steel-blue "shooter" in each hand, stole the payroll from
a levee work camp, and then was "blowed down 'tween two moun-
tins" by a host of "depitties." The emphasis in this work song, still
shouted out by railroad gangs and convict-lease crews, is not on
Laz'us' brief moment of heroism but on Laz'us' sister who could
not go to her brother's funeral because "she had no shoes, Lawd,
Lawd, she had no shoes."

In the 20th century, the Black man's literary protest has deepened
and broadened and, in some instances, become quite humanistic in
tone. This latter development has taken place even as the Black
man's social and economic problems have multiplied and intensified in the sprawling urban ghettoes and the militant tone of his
literary protest has become more strident and hostile. Two instances
of protest with a humanistic emphasis are found in the two poems
that marked a new era in Black poetic expression—Margaret
Walker's "For My People" and Melvin Tolson's "Dark Symphony."
Both poems vigorously protest the Black man's social, political, and
economic lot and both have a verbal brilliance that is still poetically
captivating. What is interesting is the note of humanistic concern
that emerges in each poem. "For My People," first published by
Miss Walker in 1937 and then selected as the title poem for her
prize-winning 1942 volume, sounds the hope that Black people, although "distressed and disturbed and deceived and devoured,"
will help "to fashion a world that will hold all / the people all
the faces all the adams and eves. . . ." Similarly, Tolson's "Dark
Symphony," winner of the National Poetry Prize in 1940, closes
with the humanistic assertion that, as Black people advance through

and across their own special racial barricades, they will join and advance with "the Peoples of the World." Admittedly, each poem was written during a period in which world-wide pain, sorrow, and affliction were tangibly evident, and few could isolate the Black man's dilemma from humanity's dilemma during the depression years or during the war years. Nevertheless, it is of some interest to note how racial protest in each poem shifts to a concern for the "Peoples of the World"—for "all the adams and eves."

Beyond these two examples there are few, if any, strong expressions of humanistic protest in Black poetry during the decade of the 1940's. As the decade drew to a close, the star of Gwendolyn Brooks had fully risen, but her poetry in *Street in Bronzeville* and *Annie Allen* was devoted to small, carefully cerebrated, terse portraits of the Black urban poor. The very existence of the characters she presents is both proof and cause for racial protest, but Miss Brooks handles all with a well-disciplined aesthetic detachment and "apoplectic ice." At this point, there is no rhetorical involvement with causes, racial or otherwise. Indeed, there is no need, for each character, so neatly and precisely presented, is a racial protest in itself and a symbol of some sharply etched human dilemma. This fitted in very well with the literary mood of the late 1940's. Both Black and white critics had begun to look askance at the idea of literature as a vehicle for protest; and, after the publication of James Baldwin's essay, "Everybody's Protest Novel," in the *Partisan Review* in 1949, the critical discussion about protest in Black literature assumed some focus as a dialogue between two groups of Black writers. On one side were Baldwin and many articulate literary academicians who believed that Black writers should be more concerned with artistic craftsmanship and universal themes and less concerned with specific protest over the Black man's lot. On the opposing side were Richard Wright, Chester Himes, and other literary figures who believed that all great literature was written to protest some aspect of the human condition and that Black writers need not be any exception. A man, they argued, had to write out of his experience; for, as Arthur Miller wrote, "the fish is in the water and the water is in the fish"; if a man is hungry and rejected and angry, he will write a poem or a novel about hunger, rejection, and anger.

Fortunately, events of the 1950's—the emergence of Malcolm X

and the creed of Black separatism and new directions in the fight
for integration under the inspiring leadership and moral idealism
of Martin Luther King, Jr.—solved the problem about whether the
Black creative writer could turn his literary ploughshare into a
sword of protest. The events of the time—the marches, the speeches,
the deaths, the confrontations with police dogs and spouting fire-
hoses—left him no choice. By 1960 the dialogue of the 1940's about
protest was as anachronistic as the ancient Platonic *caveat* that too
much protest from men of literature might topple the state. Under
these favoring circumstances, the Black man's creative energies became explicitly involved with the fight for minority civil rights, and
Black poets developed a rhetoric of protest and racial confrontation
which was relevant for the times. Much of the protest reflects the
anger of the frustrated revolutionary or the racial chauvinism of
the Black separatist, but in some poets there is the note of humanistic
protest found in Tolson and Margaret Walker a generation earlier.
Gwendolyn Brooks' "Riders to the Blood-Red Wrath," for instance,
ends with the racially self-confident assertion that the American
Black man's long, bloody, and "continuing" Calvary gives him
unique insights about man's inhumanity to man. Her Black Every-
man speaks:

> But my detention and my massive stain,
> And my distortion and my Calvary
> I grind into a little lorgnette
> Most slyly: to read man's inhumanity.
> And I remark my Matter is not all.
> Man's chopped in China, in India indented.
> From Israel what's Arab is resented.

Miss Brooks' spokesman then concludes that Black America will
"Star, and esteem all that which is of woman / Human and hardly
human." Indeed, the world will be revolutionized for love by Black
America, for out of the Black man's struggle will come the renewal
of "Democracy and Christianity."

In the poetry of those young Black writers who have emerged
within the past five years, the note of humanistic protest is not as
strongly and as clearly stated as one finds in "Riders to the Blood-
Red Wrath." There are reasons for this. Gwendolyn Brooks' poem
expresses the Christian idealism of Martin Luther King, Jr. and her
enthusiastic endorsement of his "contretemps-for-love." But in April,

1968 this great and noble leader was cut down by an assassin's bullet to join an ever-lengthening list of assassination victims in a death-riddled decade. Indeed, it is something of a minor miracle that one finds in the poetry of Sonia Sanchez, Nikki Giovanni, or Don Lee any expression of humanistic concern whatsoever. For as the decade of the searing Sixties ended, the world of the young Black poet provided nothing for self-exultation, unmasked laughter, or unfettered joy. It was the kind of world that Etheridge Knight writes about from his Indiana prison cell in his poem "On Universalism":

> I see no single thread
> That binds me one to all;
> Why even common dead
> Men took the single fall.
>
> No universal laws
> Of human misery
> Create a common cause
> Or common history
> That ease black people's pains
> Nor break black people's chains.

Nevertheless, in some of the poetry of recent young Black writers there is a broad humanistic concern that breaks through the cloud-cover of confrontation rhetoric to pin-point the evils of the times, to subject these to trenchant poetical analysis, and to pronounce their desperate remedies for mankind's moral and spiritual salvation.

The world-wide plague of drug addiction is one area of humanistic concern for the young Black poet. In the suburbs and in legislative councils the official term is drug abuse, but to Sonia Sanchez and the Black community it is the "wite death." If not checked, it will destroy all of the "brothas and sistuhs" everywhere. This is the subject of Sonia Sanchez' "Blk Chant":

> we programmed fo death
> die/en
>     each day the man
>            boy
> plans our death
>         with short bread
> for short sighted minds
> with junk to paralyze our
> blk limbs

Especially does Sonia Sanchez believe that the "wite death" will destroy love. She writes:

> i wud not be yo woman
> & see u disappear
>     each day
> befo my eyes
>     and know yo
> reappearance
>    to be
>     a one
>      nite stand.
> no man
>   blk
>   lovers  cannot live
> in wite powder that removes
> them from they blk selves
>      cannot ride
> majestic wite horses
>     in a machine age.

The real tragedy for Miss Sanchez is the entrapment of the "young brothas and sistuhs" who look "so cool" in their "wite highs" on every "blk st in wite amurica"; she pleads with them to "c'mon down from yo white highs an live." The alternative is the death of all the young warriors, the death of love, and the death of change and revolution.

The fight against the "wite death" is a desperate "got-to-be" if urban civilization, white and Black, is to survive. Occasionally, America's young Black poets also express their "ought-to-be's," and here their humanism or their belief in building a better world is obvious. First, one must or ought to begin "the real work" of building families that are strong and stable; "let us begin . . . now," says Sonia Sanchez, "while our / children still / remember us and loooove." More important is the need to change the system that enslaves and imprisons and ultimately destroys. What is needed to accomplish this kind of revolutionary change is not violence, anger, or rage; what is needed are political astuteness and moral power. Only through being astute and making the right moral decisions can men, writes Sonia Sanchez, achieve the discipline, "learnen," love and power "to destroy the Beast / who inslaves us." And if love is to be expressed "in communal ways" and if there is to be a real moral revolution, Black people will have to take the lead in seeing to it that "no blk person starves or is killed on a 'saturday nite corner.' "

Finally, it is Don L. Lee—the carping, cynical ironist and master of the satirical thrust—who most explicitly exhorts the beautiful people of the world to retrieve "the unimpossibility" by rescuing the world from woe, deceit and inhumanity and from the "un-people" who created that world. So, in his final poem in *Don't Cry, Scream,* Lee says to the "beautiful people":

> come
> brothers / fathers / sisters / mothers / sons / daughters
>            *       *       *
>
> walk on. smile a little
> yeah, that's it beautiful people
> move on in . . .
>            to return
> this earth into the hands of human beings.

In *We Walk the Way of the New World* (1970) the need for change and a pattern of humanistic protest to achieve that change are discussed in the Preface. Lee writes:

> We need innovators and producers of positive change. The older generation's resistance to change is natural; so how do we change without alienating them? How can we reduce if not completely elimi-nate all the negativism, pettiness and cliquishness that exist and are so damaging? . . . How can we create a common consciousness, based on a proven humanism—as we stop trying to prove our humanism to those who are inhuman?

Accordingly, readers of his "New World Poems" in this volume are charged to "change" and "create a climate for change." In the title poem of the volume, Lee closes with a description of his apocalyptical vision of a world in which "our dreams are realities" and all the "ought-to-be's" have been satisfied. In such a world there will be no "dangercourse" to run; men will walk "in cleanli-ness"

> down state st / or Fifth Ave.
> & wicked apartment buildings shake
> as their windows announce our presence

> as we jump into the interior
> & cut the day's evil away.

In the new world that Don Lee envisions, "realpeople" and the beautiful people become "the owners of the New World," but they

> will run it as unowners
> for
> we will live in it too
> & will want to be remembered
> as     realpeople.

Many critics and students of poetry find the poetry of our new young Black poets abrasive in tone, offensive in style, and too full of anger and hate. But like other Black poets in other times, these new Black poets are merely being responsive to the conditions under which they have had to live and write. In order to cope with the world's massive disorders and calamities, they developed a rhetoric of racial confrontation and used that rhetoric in a righteously angry "speak-out" against a dishonest and immoral Establishment. In the process, some poets have paused to reflect on this Establishment, and a few have dared to protest for change and renewal in this Establishment. These few are part of a long tradition in Black poetry, for the roots of the tradition of protest run deep in the Black man's history. In this sense, the circle from George Moses Horton to Don L. Lee is unbroken. Each Black poet has attempted, through his own special pattern of protest, to express a Black humanism that would speak to the inhumanity of his times.

# Notes on the Editor and Contributors

DONALD B. GIBSON is Professor of English at the University of Connecticut. He is author of *The Fiction of Stephen Crane* (1969) and has edited *Five Black Writers: Essays on Wright, Ellison, Baldwin, Hughes and LeRoi Jones* (1970), and *Black and White: Stories of American Life* (1971).

RICHARD K. BARKSDALE, formerly Dean of the College of Liberal Arts, Atlanta University, is presently Professor of English at the University of Illinois and coeditor of *Black Writers of America: A Comprehensive Anthology* (1972).

EUGENIA W. COLLIER teaches English at the Community College of Baltimore. Critic, reviewer, and writer of fiction, she is coeditor of an anthology of black writers forthcoming from New York University Press.

ARTHUR P. DAVIS, a pioneer in the study of black writers, is Professor of English at Howard University. He is coeditor of *The Negro Caravan* (1939), the first comprehensive volume of literature by black writers. He has also coedited *Cavalcade: Negro American Writing from 1760 to the Present* (1971), which is a revised version of *The Negro Caravan*.

CHARLES T. DAVIS, Professor of English at Yale University, has edited E. A. Robinson's *Selected Early Poems and Letters*, Lucy Larcom's *A New England Girlhood*, and *On Being Black: Writings of Afro-Americans from Frederick Douglass to the Present*. He is presently at work on a monograph on the Harlem Renaissance.

JAMES A. EMANUEL, Professor of English at the City College of New York, is author of *Langston Hughes* (1967) and many articles on black writers. His poetry has been frequently anthologized, and he is coeditor of *Dark Symphony: Negro Literature in America*.

LEE A. JACOBUS is Associate Professor of English at the University of Connecticut. His criticism is principally on seventeenth-century authors and John Milton. He is author of a forthcoming study of John Cleveland.

MONTGOMERY WORDSWORTH KING, Professor of English at Southern University, is editor of the *Southern Creative and Research Bulletin*. He is

165

author of *Questionmark* (among other novels) and has published numerous articles, poems, and short stories.

R. RODERICK PALMER is Professor and Chairman of the Department of English at Southern University. He is the author of numerous articles in educational journals.

DUDLEY RANDALL is a well-known and frequently anthologized poet who founded and operates the most significant outlet for the writing of black authors, the Broadside Press in Detroit.

J. SAUNDERS REDDING, Professor of English at Cornell University, was an early contributor to the study of black writers with his book, *To Make a Poet Black* (1939). He has been a director of the National Endowment for the Humanities and has recently coedited *Cavalcade: Negro American Writing from 1760 to the Present* (1971).

CLYDE TAYLOR teaches English at the University of California at Los Angeles. A Blake Scholar, he has written articles on Blake and on several black writers.

# Selected Bibliography

The following is a fairly full guide to the scholarly and critical work of this century on the poetry of black writers. The first section contains works of a general character; the second contains studies devoted to individual poets. The selection of writers in the second section has been determined necessarily by the amount and quality of scholarly and critical work available. Hence some good and reasonably well-known poets, Margaret Walker and Margaret Danner, for example, and younger poets, such as Don L. Lee and Sonia Sanchez, have been excluded simply because there is as yet little or no writing about them. Reviews and newspaper and magazine articles have for the most part been omitted unless they are of particular significance.

## General

1. Aubert, Alvin. "Black American Poetry: Its Language and the Folk Tradition." *Black Academy Review* 1 and 2 (Spring–Summer):408–16.

2. Bailey, Leaonead. *Broadside Authors: A Biographical Directory.* Detroit: Broadside Press, 1971.

3. Barksdale, Richard K. "Trends in Contemporary Poetry." *Phylon* 19 (1958):408–16.

4. ———. "Urban Crisis and the Black Poetic Avant-Garde." *Negro American Literature Forum* 3:40–44.

5. Bell, Bernard W. "New Black Poetry: A Double-Edged Sword. *College Language Association Journal* 15 (September, 1971):37–43.

6. Bennet, M. W. "Negro Poets." *Negro History Bulletin* 9 (1946):171–72.

7. Berceanu, Vera. "The Harlem Renaissance." *Contemporanul* 10 (July, 1970):9.

8. Berger, Art. "Negroes with Pens." *Mainstream* 16 (July, 1963):3–6.

9. "Black Writers' Views on Literary Lions and Values." Symposium in *Negro Digest* 17 (January, 1968):10–48, 81–89.

10. Bland, Edward. "Racial Bias and Negro Poetry." *Phylon* 53 (1944): 328–33.

11. Bone, Robert. "American Negro Poets: A French View." *Tri-Quarterly* No. 4 (1965):185–95.

12. Bontemps, Arna. "American Negro Poetry." *Crisis* 70 (1963):509.

13. ———. "The Black Renaissance of the Twenties." *Black World* 20 (January, 1970):118–26.

14. ———. "The Harlem Renaissance." *Saturday Review of Literature* 30 (March 22, 1947):12–13, 44.

15. ———. "Negro Poets, Then and Now." *Phylon* 11 (1950):355–60.

16. Braithwaite, William S. "The Negro in Literature." *Crisis* 28 (September, 1924):204–10.

17. ———. "Some Contemporary Poets of the Negro Race." *Crisis* 17 (1919): 275–80.

18. Brawley, Benjamin. "The Negro Literary Renaissance." *Southern Workman* 56 (April, 1927):177–80.

19. Breman, Paul. "Poetry into the Sixties." *The Black American Writer*. Edited by C. W. E. Bigsby. Deland, Florida: Everett/Edwards, Inc., 1969.

20. Bronz, Stephen H. "Roots of Negro Racial Consciousness," *The 1920's: Harlem Renaissance Authors*. New York: Libra Publishers, Inc., 1964 (James Weldon Johnson; Countee Cullen; Claude McKay).

21. Brooks, Gwendolyn. "Poets Who Are Negro." *Phylon* 11 (1950):312.

22. Brooks, A. Russel. "The Motif of Dynamic Change in Black Revolutionary Poetry." *College Language Association Journal* 1 (September, 1971):7–17.

23. Brown, Sterling. *Negro Poetry and Drama*. Washington, D.C.: Associates in Negro Folk Education, 1937.

24. ———. *Outline for the Study of the Poetry of American Negroes*. New York: Associates in Negro Folk Education, 1931.

25. Calverton, V. F. "The Advance of Negro Literature." *Opportunity* 4 (February, 1926):54–55.

26. Cartey, Wilfred. "Four Shadows of Harlem." *Negro Digest* 18 (August, 1969):22–25.

27. Chapman, Abraham. "Black Poetry Today." *Arts in Society* (University of Wisconsin) 5 (1968):401–8.

28. Charters, Samuel B. *The Poetry of the Blues*. New York: Oak Publishers, 1963.

29. Collier, Eugenia. "Heritage from Harlem." *Black World* 19 (November, 1970):52–59.

30. Cook, Mercer, and Stephen E. Henderson, *The Militant Black Writer in Africa and the United States*. Madison: University of Wisconsin Press, 1969.

31. Davis, Arthur P. "The New Poetry of Black Hate." *College Language Association Journal* 14 (June, 1970):382–91.

32. Daykin, Walter I. "Race Consciousness in Negro Poetry." *Sociology and Social Research* 20 (1936):98–105.

33. Dreer, Herman. *American Literature by Negro Authors*. New York: The Macmillan Co., 1950.

34. Echeruo, M. J. C. "American Negro Poetry." *Phylon* 24 (1963):62–68.

35. Ellison, Martha. "Velvet Voices Feed on Bitter Fruit: A Study of American Negro Poetry." *Poet and Critic* 4 (Winter, 1967–68):39–49.

36. Ely, Effie Smith. "American Negro Poetry." *The Christian Century* 40 (1923):366–67.

37. Emanuel, James A. "Blackness Can: A Quest for Aesthetics." *The Black Aesthetic*. Edited by Addison Gayle, Jr. Garden City, New York: Doubleday and Company, Inc., 1971.

38. Fabio, Sarah Webster. "Tripping with Black Writing." *The Black Aesthetic*. Edited by Addison Gayle, Jr. Garden City, New York: Doubleday and Company, Inc., 1971.

39. Furay, Michael. "Africa in Negro American Poetry to 1929." *African Literature Today* 2:32–41.

40. Garrett, DeLois. "Dream Motif in Contemporary Negro Poetry." *English Journal* 49 (1970):767–70.

41. Garrett, Naomi M. "Racial Motifs in Contemporary American and French Negro Poetry." *West Virginia University Philological Papers* 14 (1963):80–101.

42. Gayle, Addison, Jr., ed. *The Black Aesthetic*. Garden City, New York: Doubleday and Company, Inc., 1971.

43. ———. "Cultural Strangulation: Black Literature and the White Aesthetic." *Negro Digest* 18 (September, 1969):32–39.

44. Gibson, Donald B., ed. *Five Black Writers*. New York: New York University Press, 1970.

45. Glicksberg, Charles. "The Alienation of Negro Literature." *Phylon* 11 (1950):49–58.

46. ——. "Negro Poets and the American Tradition." *Antioch Review* 6 (1946):243–53.

47. Good, Charles Hamilton. "The First American Negro Literary Movement." *Opportunity* 10 (1932):69–76.

48. Gregory, Horace, and Zaturenska, Marya. "The Negro Poet in America." *A History of American Poetry, 1900–1940.* New York: Harcourt, Brace and Co., 1964.

49. Heath, Phoebe Anne. "Negro Poetry as an Historical Record." *Vassar Journal of Undergraduate Studies* 3 (May, 1928):34–52.

50. Hill, Herbert, ed. *Anger and Beyond: The Negro Writer in the United States.* New York: Harper and Row Publishers, 1966.

51. Horne, Frank S. "Black Verse." *Opportunity* 2 (1924):330–32.

52. Huggins, Nathan Irvin. *Harlem Renaissance.* New York: Oxford University Press, 1971.

53. Jackson, August V. "The Renaissance of Negro Literature 1922 to 1929." Unpublished Master's Thesis, Atlanta, Georgia: Atlanta University, June, 1936.

54. Johnson, Charles S. "Jazz Poetry and Blues." *Carolina* 57 (May, 1928): 16–20.

55. Johnson, James Weldon. "Preface." *The Book of American Negro Poetry.* James Weldon Johnson ed. New York: Harcourt, Brace and Co., 1931:3–48.

56. Jones, LeRoi (Imamu Amiri Baraka). "The Black Aesthetic." *Negro Digest* 18 (September, 1969):5–6.

57. Kerlin, Robert T. "Conquest by Poetry." *The Southern Workman* 56 (1927):282–84.

58. ——. *Contemporary Poetry of the Negro.* Hampton, Virginia: Press of the Hampton Normal and Agricultural Institute, 1921.

59. ——. "Present-Day Negro Poets." *The Southern Workman* 69 (1920): 543–48.

60. ——. "Singers of New Songs." *Opportunity* 4 (1926):162–64.

61. Kgositsile, W. Keorapetse. "Paths to the Future." *The Black Aesthetic.* (*See* General Bibliography No. 42.)

62. Kilgore, James C. "Toward the Dark Tower." *Black World* 19 (June, 1970):14–17.

63. Killens, John O. "Another Time When Black Was Beautiful." *Black World* 20 (January, 1971):20–36. (Harlem Renaissance).

64. Kjersmeier, Carl. "Negroes as Poets." *Crisis* 30 (1925):186–89.

65. Lee, Don L. "Black Critics." *Black World* 19 (November, 1970):24–30.

66.    ———. "Black Poetry: Which Direction?" *Negro Digest* 17 (September–October, 1968):27–32.

67.    ———. *Dynamite Voices: Black Poets of the 1960's.* Detroit: Broadside Press, 1971.

68.    ———. "Toward a Definition: Black Poetry of the Sixties (After LeRoi Jones)." (*See* General Bibliography No. 42.)

69.    Locke, Alain. "The Message of the Negro Poets." *Carolina* 57 (May, 1928):5–15.

70.    Lowenfels, Walter. "Black Renaissance." *American Dialog* 5 (1968): 30–31. (On contemporary black poets)

71.    Monroe, Harriet. "Negro Sermon Poetry." *Phylon* 30 (1923):291–93.

72.    Moore, Gerald. "Poetry in the Harlem Renaissance." *The Black American Writer.* Edited by C. W. E. Bigsby. Deland, Florida: Everett/Edwards, Inc., 1969. Vol. 2:67–76.

73.    Moore, Rayburn S. "Thomas Dun's English. A Forgotten Contributor to the Development of Negro Dialect Verse in the 1870's." *American Literature.* 33 (1961):72–75.

74.    Morpurgo, J. E. "American Poetry." *Fortnightly.* 168 (July, 1947): 16–24.

75.    Morton, Lena Beatrice. *Negro Poetry in America.* Boston: Stratford Co., 1925.

76.    "The Negro Writer and His Relationship to His Roots." *The American Negro Writer and His Roots.* New York: American Society of African Culture, 1960.

77.    "The New Negro in Literature (1925–55)." *The New Negro Thirty Years Afterwards.* Washington, D.C.: Howard University Press, 1955: 57–72.

78.    Palmer, R. Roderick. "The Poetry of Three Revolutionists: Don L. Lee, Sonia Sanchez and Nikki Giovanni." *College Language Association Journal* 15 (September, 1971):25–36.

79.    Pool, Rosey. "The Discovery of American Negro Poetry." *Freedomways* 3 (1963):46–51.

80.    Portelli, Allesandro. "Cultura poetica afro-americana." *Studi Americane* (Roma) 14 (1968):401–29.

81.    Preminger, Alex; Frank H. Warnhand; and O. B. Hardison, Jr., eds. "Negro Poetry." *Encyclopedia of Poetry and Poetics.* Princeton: Princeton University Press, 1965.

82.    Ramsaran, J. A. "The 'Twice-Born' Artists' Silent Revolution." *Black World* 20 (May, 1971):58–68.

83. Randall, Dudley. "The Black Aesthetic in the Thirties, Forties, and Fifties." (*See* General Bibliography No. 42.)

84. ———. "Ubi Sunt and Hic Sum." *Negro Digest* 14 (September, 1965): 73–76.

85. ———. "White Poet, Black Critic." *Negro Digest* 14 (February, 1965): 46–48.

86. Redding, Saunders J. "American Negro Literature." *American Scholar* 18 (Spring, 1949):137–48.

87. ———. *To Make a Poet Black*. Chapel Hill: University of North Carolina Press, 1939. (*See also* General Bibliography No. 76.)

88. Redmond, Eugene B. "The Black American Epic: Its Roots, Its Writers." *The Black Scholar* 2 (January, 1971):15–22.

89. Rodgers, Carolyn M. "Black Poetry—Where It's At." *Negro Digest* 18 (September, 1969):7–16.

90. Rollins, Charlemae. *Famous American Negro Poets*. New York: Dodd, Mead, and Co., 1965. (Informative for younger readers.)

91. Taussig, Charlotte E. "The New Negro as Revealed in His Poetry." *Opportunity* 5 (1927):108–11.

92. Thurman, Wallace. "Negro Poets and Their Poetry." *Bookman* 67 (1928):555–61.

93. ———. "The Umbra Poets." *Mainstream* 16 (July, 1963):7–13.

94. "The Underground Pursuit of Fury." *Time* 95 (April 6, 1970):98–100.

95. Wagner, Jean. *Les poètes nègres des Etats-Unis: Le sentiment racial et religieux dans la poésie de P. L. Dunbar à L. Hughes*. Paris: Istra, 1963.

96. Walker, Margaret. "New Poets." *Phylon* 11 (1950):345–54.

97. White, Newman. "American Negro Poetry." *South Atlantic Quarterly* 20 (1921):304–22.

98. ———. "Racial Feeling in Negro Poetry." *South Atlantic Quarterly* 21 (1922):14–21.

99. Williams, John A. "The Harlem Renaissance: Its Artists, Its Impact, Its Meaning," *Black World* 20 (January, 1971):17–18.

100. Work, Monroe N. "The Spirit of Negro Poetry." *The Southern Workman* 37 (1908):73–77.

101. Wright, Richard. "Litterature noire américaine." *Les Temps Moderne* 4 (1948):193–221.

# Individual Authors

BROOKS, GWENDOLYN

1. Bird, Leonard G. "Gwendolyn Brooks: Educator Extraordinaire." *Discourse* 12:158–66.

2. Brown, Frank London. "Chicago's Great Lady of Poetry." *Negro Digest* 11 (December, 1962): 53–57.

3. Crockett, J. "An Essay on Gwendolyn Brooks." *Negro Historical Bulletin* 19 (1955):37–39.

4. Cutler, B. "Long Reach, Strong Speech." *Poetry* 103 (1964): 388–89.

5. Davis, Arthur P. "The Black-and-Tan Motif in the Poetry of Gwendolyn Brooks." *College Language Association Journal* 6 (1962):90–97.

6. ———. "Gwendolyn Brooks: A Poet of the Unheroic." *College Language Association Journal* 7 (1963):114–25.

7. Emanuel, James A. "A Note on the Future of Negro Poetry." *Negro American Literature Forum* 1 (Fall, 1967):2–3.

8. Kunitz, Stanley. "Bronze by Gold." *Poetry* 126 (1950): 52–56.

9. Rollins, Charlemae. *Famous American Negro Poets.* (*See* General Bibliography No. 90.)

10. Stavros, George. "An Interview with Gwendolyn Brooks." *Contemporary Literature* 11:1–20.

11. *Twentieth Century Authors,* First Supplement (1955).


CULLEN, COUNTEE

12. Bontemps, Arna. "Countee Cullen, American Poet." *The People's Voice* 5 (January 26, 1946):52–53.

13. ———. "The Harlem Renaissance." (*See* General Bibliography No. 14.)

14. Bronz, Stephen H. "Roots of Negro Racial Consciousness." (*See* General Bibliography No. 20.)

15. Collier, Eugenia. "I Do Not Marvel, Countee Cullen." *College Language Association Journal* 11 (September, 1967):73–87.

16. Daniel, Walter C. "Countee Cullen as Literary Critic." *College Language Association Journal* 3 (March, 1971):281–90.

17. Davis, Arthur. "The Alien-and-Exile Theme in Countee Cullen's Racial Poems." *Phylon* 14 (1953):390–400.

18. Dinger, Helen. "A Study of Countee Cullen with Emphasis on His Poetical Works." Unpublished Master's Thesis, Columbia University, 1953.

19. Dodson, Owen. "Countee Cullen (1903–1946)." *Phylon* 7 (1946):19–21.

20. Dorsey, David F., Jr. "Countee Cullen's Use of Greek Mythology." *College Language Association Journal* 13 (1969):68–77.

21. Ferguson, Blanche E. *Countee Cullen and the Harlem Renaissance.* New York: Dodd, Mead and Co., 1968.

22. Gloster, Hugh M. *Negro Voices in American Fiction.* Chapel Hill: University of North Carolina Press, 1948.

23. Huggins, Nathan Irvin. *Harlem Renaissance.* (*See* General Bibliography No. 52.) (Countee Cullen 204–14 and passim.)

24. Johnson, Charles, ed. "Countee Cullen." *Source Material for Patterns of Negro Segregation.* Vol. 8. New York: Schomburg Collection.

25. Locke, Alain, ed. *Four Negro Poets.* New York: Simon and Schuster, 1927 (Works of Claude McKay, Countee Cullen, Jean Toomer, and Langston Hughes with critical commentaries by the editor).

26. Perry, Margaret. "A Bio-Bibliography of Countee P. Cullen." Unpublished Master's Thesis, Catholic University of America, 1959.

27. Redding, Saunders J. *To Make a Poet Black.* (*See* General Bibliography No. 87).

28. Reimherr, Beulah. "Countee Cullen: A Biographical and Critical Study." Unpublished Master's Thesis, College Park, Maryland: University of Maryland, 1960.

29. ———. "Race Consciousness in Countee Cullen's Poetry." *Susquehanna University Studies* 7 (February, 1963):65–82.

30. Robb, Izetta W. "From the Darker Side." *Opportunity* 4 (1926):381–82.

31. Smith, Robert. "The Poetry of Countee Cullen." *Phylon* 11 (1950):216–21.

32. Turner, Darwin T. *In a Minor Chord: Three Afro-American Writers and Their Search for Identity.* Carbondale: Southern Illinois University Press, 1971 (Jean Toomer, Countee Cullen, and Zora Neale Hurston.)

33. Webster, Harvey. "A Difficult Career." *Poetry* 70 (1947):22–25.

34. Woodruff, Bertram. "The Poetic Philosophy of Countee Cullen." *Phylon* 1 (1940):213–23.

HAYDEN, ROBERT E.

35. Galler, D. "Three Recent Volumes." *Poetry* 110 (1967):268.

36. *Negro Historical Bulletin* 21 (October, 1957):15. (Biographical sketch, portrait).

37. Pool, Rosey E. "Robert Hayden: Poet Laureate." *Negro Digest* 15 (June, 1966):39–43.


HUGHES, LANGSTON

38. Allen, Samuel W. "Negritude and Its Relevance to the American Negro Writer." (See General Bibliography No. 76:8–20.)

39. Avery, Verna. "Langston Hughes: Crusader." *Opportunity* 18 (1940): 363–64.

40. "Birth of a Poet." Milwaukee *Journal* (February 5, 1945). See also *Negro Digest* (April, 1945):41–42.

41. Bontemps, Arna. "The Two Harlems." *American Scholar* 14 (Spring, 1945): 167–73.

42. Brooks, Gwendolyn. "Langston Hughes." (Editorial) *Nation* 205 (July 3, 1967):7.

43. Burroughs, Margaret. "Langston Hughes Lives!" *Negro Digest* 16 (September, 1967): 59–60.

44. Calverton, V. F. "This Negro." *Nation* 131 (August 6, 1930):157–58.

45. Carmen, Y. "Langston Hughes: Poet of the People." *International Literature* No. 1 (1939):192–94.

46. Cartey, Wilfred. "Four Shadows of Harlem." (*See* General Bibliography No. 26).

47. Cullen, Countee. "Our Book Shelf: Poet on Poet." *Opportunity* 4 (1926):73.

48. Davis, Arthur P. "Langston Hughes: Cool Poet." *College Language Association Journal* 11 (1967):280–96.

49. ———. "The Harlem of Langston Hughes' Poetry." *Phylon* 13 (1952): 276–83.

50. Diakhate, Lamune. "Langston Hughes, conquérant de l'espoir." *Presence Africaine* (1967):38–46.

51. Dickinson, Donald C. *A Bio-Bibliography of Langston Hughes: 1902–1967*. Hamden, Conn.: Shoestring Press, 1967.

52. DuBois, W. E. B., and Alain Locke. "The Younger Literary Movement." *Crisis* 27 (February, 1924):161–63.

53. Ellison, Martha. "Velvet Voices Feed on Bitter Fruit: A Study of American Negro Poetry." (*See* General Bibliography.)

54. Emanuel, James A. *Langston Hughes.* New York: Twayne, 1967.

55. Emanuel, James A., and Theodore L. Gross, eds. *Dark Symphony: Negro Literature in America.* New York: The Free Press, 1968:191–203.

56. Embre, Edwin R. "Langston Hughes: Shakespeare in Harlem." *13 Against the Odds.* Port Washington, New York: Kennikat, 1967 (Biographies: originally published in 1944).

57. Evans, Mari. "I Remember Langston." *Negro Digest* 16 (September, 1967):36.

58. Farrison, Edward W. "*The Panther and the Lash:* Poems of Our Times." *College Language Association Journal* 11 (1968):259–61 (A review of *The Panther and the Lash*).

59. Fontaine, William T. "The Negro Continuum from Dominant Wish to Collective Act." *A Forum* 3, iv/4, i (1968):63–96 (Dunbar, DuBois, Hughes, Wright, Ellison).

60. Gibson, Donald B., ed. *Five Black Writers.* (*See* General Bibliography No. 44.)

61. ———. "The Good Black Poet and the Good Gray Poet: The Poetry of Hughes and Whitman." (*See* No. 84 below.)

62. "Harlem Literati in the Twenties." *Saturday Review of Literature.* 20 (June, 1940):13–14.

63. Holmes, Eugene C. "Langston Hughes: Philosopher–Poet." *Freedomways* 8 (Spring, 1968):144–51.

64. Hudson, Theodore R. "Langston Hughes' Last Volume of Verse." *College Language Association Journal* 11 (1967):345–48 (A review of *The Panther and the Lash*).

65. Huggins, Nathan Irvin. *Harlem Renaissance.* (*See* General Bibliography No. 52):65–69 and passim.

66. Hughes, Langston. "My Adventures as a Social Poet." *Phylon* 8 (1947):205–13.

67. ———. "The Negro Artist and the Racial Mountain." *Nation* 122 (1926):692–94.

68. Isaacs, Harold R. "Five Writers and Their African Ancestors: Part I." *Phylon* 21 (1960):243–65 (J. Baldwin, R. Ellison, L. Hansberry, L. Hughes, and R. Wright).

69. Jackson, Blyden. "An Essay in Criticism." *Phylon* 11 (1950):338–43.

70. Johnson, Charles S. "Jazz, Poetry and Blues." (*See* General Bibliography No. 54.)

71. Kent, George E. "Langston Hughes and Afro American Folk and Cultural Tradition." (*See* No. 84 below.)

72. King, Woody, Jr. "Remembering Langston: A Poet of Black Theater." *Negro Digest* 18 (April, 1969):27–32, 95–96.

73. Kramer, Aaron. "Robert Burns and Langston Hughes." *Freedomways* 8 (1968):159–66.

74. Larkin, Margaret. "A Poet for the People." *Opportunity* 5 (1927):84–85.

75. Liberman, Laurence. "Poetry Chronicle." *Poetry* 112 (August, 1968): 339–40.

76. Littlejohn, David. *Black on White: A Critical Survey of Writing by American Negroes.* New York: Grossman Publisher, Inc., 1966:51–55, 144–47.

77. Locke, Alain, ed. *Four Negro Poets.* (*See* Countee Cullen above, No. 25.)

78. Long, Richard A. "Poems from Black Africa." *College Language Association Journal* 7 (December, 1963):176.

79. Lucas, Bob. "The Poet Who Invented Soul." *Los Angeles Sentinel* (June 8, 1967):D–1.

80. MacLeod, Norman. "The Poetry and Argument of Langston Hughes." *Crisis* 45 (1938):358–59.

81. Marcus, Steven. "The American Negro in Search of Identity." *Commentary* 16 (1953):456–63.

82. McGhee, Nancy B. "Langston Hughes: Poet in the Folk Manner." (*See* No. 85 below.)

83. Mitchell, Loften. "In Memoriam to Langston Hughes." *New York Amsterdam News* (May 27, 1967): 1, 29.

84. ———. "For Langston Hughes and Stella Holt: An Informal Memoir." *Negro Digest* 12 (1968):41–43, 74–77.

85. O'Daniel, Therman B., ed. *Langston Hughes: Black Genius, A Critical Evaluation.* New York: William Morrow and Co., Inc., 1971.

86. Peterkin, Julia. "Negro Blue and Gold." *Poetry* 31 (1927):44–47.

87. Pool, Rosey. "The Discovery of American Negro Poetry." (*See* General Bibliography No. 79):511–17.

88. Presley, James. "The American Dream of Langston Hughes." *Southwest Review* 48 (1963):380–86.

89.  Randall, Dudley. "Three Giants Gone." *Negro Digest* 16 (November, 1967):87.

90.  Redding, Saunders J. *To Make a Poet Black.* (*See* General Bibliography No. 87.)

91.  Schoell, Frank. "Un poète nègre." *Revue politique et littéraire* 20 (1929):436–38.

92.  Special Langston Hughes Number. *College Language Association Journal* 11 (June, 1968).

93.  Special Supplement on Langston Hughes. *Freedomways* 8 No. 2 (Spring, 1968).

94.  Thurman, Wallace. "Negro Poets and Their Poetry." (*See* General Bibliography No. 92.) Reprinted in Addison Gayle, ed. *Black Expression.* New York: Weybright and Talley, 1969:70–81.

95.  Wagner, Jean. (*See* General Bibliography No. 95.)

96.  Walker, Margaret. "New Poets." (*See* General Bibliography No. 96.)


JONES, LE ROI (IMAMU AMIRI BARAKA)

97.  "The Black Aesthetic." (*See* General Bibliography No. 56.).

98.  Brown, Cecil M. "Black Literature and LeRoi Jones." *Black World* 19 (July, 1970):24–31.

99.  Costello, Donald B. "LeRoi Jones: Black Man as Victim." *Commonweal* 88 (June 28, 1968):436–40.

100. Dennison, George. "The Demagogy of LeRoi Jones." *Commentary* 49 (1965):67–70.

101. Gibson, Donald B., ed. *Five Black Writers.* (*See* General Bibliography No. 44.)

102. Hughes, Langston. "That Boy LeRoi." *Chicago Defender* (January 11, 1965).

103. Jackson, Kathryn. "LeRoi Jones and the New Black Writers of the Sixties." *Freedomways* 9 (1969):232–48.

104. "The LeRoi Jones Case: Letter About a Wolf-Pack." *American Dialog* 5, i (1968):17.

105. Levertov, Denise. "Poets of the Given Ground." *Nation* 192 (October 14, 1961):251–52.

106. Lewis, Ida. "LeRoi Jones: Une interview exclusive." *Jeune Afrique* (Paris), (September):24–27.

107. Major, Clarence. "The Poetry of LeRoi Jones." *Negro Digest* 14 (March, 1965):54–56.

108. Margolies, Edward. "Prospects: LeRoi Jones?" *Native Sons.* Philadelphia and New York: J. B. Lippincott, 1968.

109. Neal, Lawrence P. "Development of LeRoi Jones." *Liberator* 6 No. 1 (January, 1966):20 (Part I), 6 No. 2 (February, 1966):18 (Part II).

110. Otten, Charlotte. "LeRoi Jones: Napalm Poet." (*See* General Bibliography No. 42.)

111. Peavy, Charles D. "Myth, Magic and Manhood in LeRoi Jones' *Madheart.*" *Studies in Black Literature* 1 (February):12–20.

112. Reed, Daphne S. "LeRoi Jones: High Priest of the Black Arts Movement." *Educational Theatre Journal* 22:53–59.

113. Resnik, H. S. "Brave New Words." *Saturday Review,* 50 (December 9, 1967):28–29.

114. Richardson, J. "Blues for Mr. Jones." *Esquire* 65 (June, 1966): 106–8.

115. Russell, Charlie. "LeRoi Jones Will Get Us All in Trouble." *Liberator* 4 No. 8 (August, 1964):18.

116. Velde, Paul. "LeRoi Jones: Pursued by the Furies." *Commonweal* 88:440–41.

117. X, Marvin, and Faruh. "Islam and Black Art: An Interview with LeRoi Jones." *Negro Digest* 18 (March, 1969):4–10, 77–80.

MC KAY, CLAUDE

118. Barton, Rebecca C. "A Long Way from Home: Claude McKay." *Witnesses for Freedom.* New York: Harper & Bros., 1948.

119. Butcher, Philip. "Claude McKay—'If We Must Die'." *Opportunity* 26 (1948):127.

120. Cartey, Wilfred. "Four Shadows of Harlem." (*See* General Bibliography No. 26.)

121. Conroy, Sister M. James, O.S.U. "Claude McKay: Negro Poet and Novelist." *Dissertation Abstracts* 29:31 29A–30A (Notre Dame).

122. Cooper, Wayne. "Claude McKay and the New Negro of the 1920's." *Phylon* 25 (1964):297–306.

123. Gloster, Hugh M. (*See* Countee Cullen above No. 22.)

124. Huggins, Nathan Irvin. *Harlem Renaissance.* (*See* General Bibliography No. 52):124–28, 214–20 and passim.

125. Jackson, Blyden. "The Essential McKay." *Phylon* 14 (1953):216–17.

126. Kaye, Jacqueline. "Claude McKay's Banjo." *Presence Africaine* 73: 165–69.

127. Kent, George E. "The Soulful Way of Claude McKay." *Black World* 20 (January, 1971):37–51.

128. Locke, Alain, ed. *Four Negro Poets.* (*See* Countee Cullen above No. 25.)

129. McKay, Claude. "A Negro to His Critics." *New York Herald Tribune Books.* March 6, 1932.

130. Redding, Saunders. *To Make a Poet Black.* (*See* General Bibliography No. 87.)

131. Smith, Robert A. "Claude McKay: An Essay in Criticism." *Phylon* 9 (1948):270–73.


TOLSON, MELVIN B.

132. Fabio, Sarah Webster. "Who Speaks Negro?" *Negro Digest* 16 (December, 1967):54–58.

133. Flasch, Joy. "Humor and Satire in the Poetry of M. B. Tolson." *Satire Newsletter* Fall, 1969.

134. McCall, Dan. "The Quicksilver Sparrow of Melvin B. Tolson." *American Quarterly* 18 (1966):538–42.

135. Randall, Dudley. "Melvin B. Tolson: Portrait of a Poet as Raconteur." *Negro Digest* 15 (January, 1966): 54–57.

136. Shapiro, Karl. "Melvin B. Tolson, Poet." *Book Week, New York Herald Tribune.* January 10, 1965. Reprinted in *Negro Digest* 14 (May, 1965):75–77.

137. Tate, Allen. "Preface to *Libretto for the Republic of Liberia.*" *Poetry* 76 (1950):216–18.

138. Thompson, D. G. "Tolson's Gallery Brings Poetry Home." *Negro History Bulletin* 29 (1965):69–70.


TOOMER, JEAN

139. Ackley, Donald G. "Theme and Vision in Jean Toomer's *Cane.*" *Studies in Black Literature* 1, i:45–65.

140. Bell, Bernard. "A Key to the Poems in *Cane.*" *College Language Association Journal* 3 (March, 1971):251–58.

141. Bontemps, Arna. "The Negro Renaissance." *Sewanee Review* 30 (March 22, 1947):12–13, 44.

142. ———. "The Negro Renaissance: Jean Toomer and the Harlem Writers of the 1920's." *Anger and Beyond*: 20–36. (*See* General Bibliography No. 50.)

143. Chase, Patricia. "The Women in *Cane.*" *College Language Association Journal* 3 (March, 1971):259–73.

144. Dillard, Mabel. "Jean Toomer: Herald of Negro Renaissance." Athens: Ohio University, 1967 (Unpublished dissertation.)

145. DuBois, W. E. B., and Alain Locke. "The Younger Literary Movement." (*See* Langston Hughes No. 52.)

146. Fullinwider, S. P. "Jean Toomer: Lost Generation, or Negro Renaissance?" *Phylon* 27 (1966):396–403.

147. Gloster, Hugh M. (*See* Countee Cullen above No. 22.)

148. Holmes, Eugene. "Jean Toomer, Apostle of Beauty." *Opportunity* 3 (1925):252–54, 60.

149. Huggins, Nathan Irvin. *Harlem Renaissance.* (*See* General Bibliography No. 52):179–87 and passim.

150. Lieber, Todd. "Design and Movement in *Cane.*" *College Language Association Journal* 13 (1969):35–50.

151. Locke, Alain. (*See* Countee Cullen above No. 25).

152. Mason, Clifford. "Jean Toomer's Black Authenticity." *Black World* 20 (January, 1971):37–51.

153. McKeever, Benjamin F. "Cane as Blues." *Negro American Literature Forum* 4:61–63.

154. Munson, Gorham. "The Significance of Jean Toomer." *Opportunity* 3 (1925):262–63.

155. Redding, Saunders J. (*See* General Bibliography No. 87.)

156. Rosenfeld, Paul. "Jean Toomer." *Men Seen.* New York: Dial Press, 1925.

157. Turner, Darwin T. "And Another Passing." *Negro American Literature Forum* (Fall, 1967):3–4.

158. ———. *In a Minor Chord: Three Afro-American Writers and Their Search for Identity.* (*See* Countee Cullen No. 32.)

159. ———. "Jean Toomer's *Cane.*" *Negro Digest* 18 (January, 1969):54–61.